Hope for the Hormonal

❖❖❖❖❖❖

Kimberly Bryan, RN, MS

Copyright © 2015, Kimberly Bryan

All rights reserved.

ISBN-13: 978-1482318371
ISBN-10: 1482318377

CONTENTS

✦✦✦✦✦

FOREWORD

SECTION 1: *MY STORY*

SECTION 2: *WORDS TO MY HORMONAL SISTER*

SECTION 3: *HOPE FOUND THROUGH HIS WORD*

Foreword

As I write this devotional book for women, I am writing from experience. For me, hormones snuck up on me and I wish I would've known then what I know now. It became a battle....a vicious battle between who I was as a christian woman and the effects that hormones were having on my mind and my body. It became a battle for my very life and the ugly side of hormones came close to winning. I've got the scars to prove it. I will frequently expose these scars to you, in hopes that it will give you insight into the battle itself. I'm not gonna lie, some of those scars break open on occasion and I am reminded that there will always be some wounds that need a healing touch.

I wrote my entire story on a blog site during the summer following my incident that took place in the Fall of 2009. My blog site, hopeforthehormonal.blogspot.com is still up and running and there have been many women that have read it and have received hope from it. I have included my story in this book, based on entries from my blog.

My time in the morning with my Lord has always been the most important time of the day for me, but it became more essential than food to me during my days of struggle. I underlined scripture, I read books, I searched for promises, I journaled. I did anything and everything I could do to receive hope. As a result, on the other side of my days of desperation, I felt led to write words of not only hope, but also words of counsel. And so, whether you are a woman that loves her time of devotion with the Lord or not, I pray that this book of encouragement gives you direction and a sense of hope as you battle hormones.

Please know that every word that is placed into this small book is not from me, but it is from my Father, my Healer, my Savior, my Lord. He has revealed some very real truths that I know He wants you to hear. I suggest that you read my entire story as you begin this book. It will allow you to catch a very close glimpse of my heart, during the pain and during the healing. Some of you may be uncertain as to what type of battle you are facing at this time in your life...you just know you don't feel like yourself. Others of you are in the heat of it and I'm sure there are days that you feel as though you are hanging on by a thread. Some of you suffer from anxiety, others of you, depression and unfortunately, many of you are plagued by both. There will be some of you that are being evaluated for mental illness, others are trying medication after medication and cannot quite seem to find one that works. Some of you are feeling guilty about the feelings you have about yourself, about your husband, your kids, or about your God. You just want to feel like yourself again. You want to feel *normal* again. There are those of you that are watching someone you love change before your very eyes. You don't know what to do to help them and sometimes it feels like they are sucking the very life out of you. Whoever you are, I pray that our Lord will hold you tightly as you face each day anew with Him. I pray that He divinely speak the words from this book on the very day you need to hear them. I pray that you hold on to the truth that you *will* get through this season of life and that you *will* become the woman that

He desires you to be *because* of it, not *in spite* of it. And most of all, I pray in the name of our Lord Jesus, that you find *His hope* in the midst of your hormones.

◆◆◆*Dedicated to Debbie*◆◆◆

I want to dedicate this book to my life-long friend, Debbie. We knew each other for almost 30 years and were the best of friends. After my breakdown, she was by my side every step of the way. She was one of my greatest encouragers and loved me through the shame and guilt, as I struggled to heal. She was the biggest supporter of my blog. She read it several times and encouraged others to read it as well. She would always tell me, "Kimmy, you just have to write a book about this. Women need to hear your story!" Oh how I wish she were here to be the first to see this book in its completion. What a joy it would be to hand her a copy of it and watch her grin from ear to ear! Debbie passed away on June 5, 2015 after a relatively short battle with cancer. *This is for you, Deb. Thank you for touching my life, thank you for making my world better, and thank you for loving me through the pain and refusing to give up on my restoration. I miss you every day.*

Section One:

My Story

The nuthouse

My eyes opened and I looked at the blank ceiling. I didn't recognize it. As I sat up, I looked around. The walls were blank, cold, white, and made of cement. There were no windows. *Oh God, please tell me I'm waking up from a very bad dream!* It was not a dream, but it certainly was a nightmare...my nightmare. Hours before, I was brought to this unfamiliar place. A lock-down psychiatric facility. Yep, a nuthouse.

It all began...

So I landed in a psych facility because I went crazy, right? Well, yes and no. I was a 49ish year old woman that never suffered from PMS a day in my life. I lived life to its absolute fullest, took on way more than I should, was passionate about my God, my family, and my friends. I had it all together! Yep, well, not so much. Something called *hormones* began to enter the Bryan household and slowly but surely took over. It snuck up on me and consumed me before I knew what happened.

Like I said, I never had a day of PMS as a young woman and in fact, gave it no merit whatsoever when I heard stories of women doing *crazy* things due to hormones. And then *life* happened. I was in the process of completing my Master's degree in nursing education, a close friend died, and I began to have cardiac complications, resulting in a catheterization. This woman that 'thrived' on stress was being eaten up by it. I began to experience anxiety and lots of it. I recognized it because I had gone through a year of supporting a dear friend that suffered from it. Little did I know that it was right around the corner for me. It came on fast and furious. I would later learn that anxiety is one of many symptoms of perimenopause and the previous months of extra stress had thrown me right into the depths of it, ready or not! Thankfully, my doctor was wise enough to call it what it was and started me on an estrogen patch. OK, I'm not exaggerating when I say that in 24 hours, I felt like a new woman! Soooo....perhaps I have been a little quick to judge those tired, worn-out women that call their life issues 'hormones'. Now I get it. I'm right there with ya, sister.

Whatever it takes

Unfortunately, the story doesn't end there. Oh how I wish that it did. What I would give to erase the next year of my life and change it up a bit. But if we are truly dedicated to wanting Christ's perfect will for our lives, then we take what comes our way and give God the glory, *right????* Well, I truly was dedicated to wanting only what Christ had in store for me. I consistently prayed, "Lord, do whatever it takes to make me into the woman of Christ You want me to be." *Whatever it takes.* Just prior to 2009, I wrote in my journal:

> **12/27/08: As I enter a new year, I pray that 2009 will be one of change. Change for me. Change for my family. May my world be forever changed because of what You choose to do in my life in 2009. Unleash Your power, that my world will be rocked, never to be the same. No more status quo, no more midstream, take us higher to new levels of intimacy with You. Choose me, Father.**

I've got to be honest here. I'm not certain I would have written that with such passion had I known just what 2009 would hold for my family and I. In fact, I'm not sure I would have written it at all! *Whatever it takes.* Hmmm....

I'm a person that writes dates and notes in my Bible next to scripture and I came across one that has particular importance. The date 3/15/09 was written next to Isaiah 43:1-3. It says, **"Fear not, for I have redeemed you. I have called you by your name. You are Mine. When you pass through the waters, I will be with you; and through the rivers, they shall not overflow you. When you walk through the fire, you shall not be burned, nor shall the flame scorch you. For I am the Lord your God, the Holy One of Israel, your Savior."** Next to the date, the words that were written, *He is preparing me for the future.* Indeed He was.

And then there were hormones....again

The pain was terrible. It was on the left side of my lower abdomen. I assumed it was an issue with my ovary. I had been diagnosed with endometriosis a number of years earlier and had several surgeries because of it, one of which resulted in the removal of my other ovary. This time, my doctor suggested a hysterectomy. Made sense to me. After all, those gems have nothing more to offer me, *right?* The surgery was scheduled for February, 2009. I was living on Ibuprofen for the pain, so the sooner the better.

All went as planned with the surgery. Indeed, endometriosis and lots of it. My recovery was uneventful and I was anxious to get back into a normal routine. Prior to the surgery, several of my *older* friends told me just how great I would feel after having a hysterectomy. As the days and weeks went by, I was feeling anything but great. I was plagued with that familiar feeling of anxiety....at its worst. I began to have hot flashes also. And just let me say, *'hot'* does not give those flashes one bit of justice! These babies were *inferno flashes*! Hot flashes are when women dab the little beads of sweat from their upper lip and fan themselves with their cute little hands. Nope. Not even close. I was waking up in sheets that were entirely drenched with sweat.. dripping! I couldn't ask my husband, Mark to get up in the middle of the night to change the sheets, so I laid towels on the bed. Not only was I running out of towels, I was also getting very little sleep. After several days, I called my surgeon and told her of my *onslaught* of symptoms. She changed the estrogen patch I had grown to know and love dearly to a pill. She said the increased dose would do the trick. A few days later, it was not better, it was worse. I called again. She increased the dose. As the days and weeks went by, the anxiety and hot flashes worsened. And I had another symptom to add to my repertoire...insomnia. It became difficult to function. I called the surgeon again. She increased my dosage to the maximum allowed. Surely this would take care of it. Several more weeks went by and the woman I once was no longer existed. An unfamiliar emotion seemed to creep into my world: insecurity. Ugghhh. How can an independent, confident woman suddenly be searching for security? I clung to my family and I clung to a few chosen friends. Although I felt safe, I was scared. I wasn't myself and all I could hope for is that those who loved me would stand by me, would accept me in my weakness, and would fight this battle with me. Little did I know what I would face in the days ahead. I reluctantly made another phone call to the doctor. Her nurse told me, "Sorry Kim, but you are on the maximum dose." *So, that's it? I just live with this?* As the weeks and months went by, those who were closest to me no longer knew me for who I once was. I didn't know myself! I cried to my Lord, I cried to my family. It was August and I was mentally and physically exhausted. I wasn't sleeping and I wasn't eating. I was a mess. A friend suggested that I go see a hormone specialist. I would do anything to feel better. Anything.

A very odd 'doc'

"Dr. Williams can't see you for several months, but his nurse practitioner can see you tomorrow." Perfect. I'm a bit partial to NP's anyway, so the next day I took my messed-up-self into a place that specializes in women's hormones. It takes some very special people to work with nothing but hormonal women, that's for certain! The usual took place: blood draw, exam, you know, all the perks that go with being a woman. In talking with the NP, I told her that I was taking an estrogen pill. She immediately looked concerned and said, "well, that will change today. I'm placing you back on an estrogen patch." *OK, whatever. Just make me feel better.*

The next day I received a phone call from the doctor's office. Well, actually, Dr. Williams himself. He said, "I need to see you in my office as soon as possible." He told me not to worry. OK, first of all, I'm a woman and second,

I'm a woman suffering from severe anxiety. Need I say more?

To say this doctor was an odd duck would be an understatement. He wore high-top red tennis shoes and sat in a little round stool with his legs criss-crossed. But I immediately liked him. I sensed his compassion from the moment he began to talk. His first words? "I wanted to see you face to face because I thought I would see a crazy woman." *Okie doke. Please continue.* "Your hormone levels are more out of whack than any I've seen and I've seen many. Your estrogen levels are 100 times the normal level. This equates to you having 40 sets of ovaries!" *Hmmmm... interesting, seeing that I don't have **any** ovaries!* He continued, "the massive amount of estrogen is causing your liver to produce proteins that try to get rid of the extra estrogen. When it cannot do so, it begins to bind to the neurotransmitters in your brain that create 'normalcy' in your thoughts and moods." He said, "to tell you the truth, I'm quite surprised that you don't feel severely depressed." *Wow.* "Well, I don't feel depressed or crazy, just extremely anxious," I told him. He proceeded to tell me that effective immediately, I would be started on an antidepressant. He said that eventually the chemicals in my brain would be affected by this overload of estrogen. *Oh super! I can hardly wait to get home to tell Mark the news! Climb aboard, family of mine, the ride's about to get even more interesting!*

Here we go

So, what in the heck caused my estrogen to surge to unbelievable levels? Evidently, large doses of the estrogen pill do not bind to the needed receptors as well as a patch or gel. Also, testosterone helps estrogen to bind to the proper receptors. Oh....one bit of info I failed to give. My testosterone level was that of a 90 year old, according to Dr. Williams. It was almost nonexistent.

The following week was uneventful, outside of anxiety, which I was learning to live with. One evening, Mark told me he was going to Homeland, our neighborhood grocery store. He would later tell me that the blank look I had on my face probably meant that I didn't hear him, which was not a rare occurrence. But, I did hear him. I just could not make sense of what he said. I responded with, "I don't know what Homeland is." I knew that I should know. I just didn't. My head felt heavy and confused. It scared both of us. Later that night, Mark and I were in the kitchen together. I said something and Mark nervously laughed. "Kim, you are talking, but you aren't making any sense." *Wow. What was happening?* The next day I called Dr. Williams' office. He wanted me to see a neurologist. But evidently, there was no urgency. They made an appointment for me for two weeks later. *Hmmm..something didn't seem right about that. Not sure why.*

Two days later, October 1st, 2009, I went on a women's retreat with my church about an hour away from home. I must say, I was a little nervous about going, not only due to my high levels of anxiety, but also because of what had taken place two days earlier. But I was determined to go. That night, I laughed, I cried, I did everything a normal woman does at a great retreat where women are gathered together in Christ. It was awesome. It was beautiful. It was just what I needed.

The next morning, I awoke and went down for breakfast where women were eating together and gabbing ninety-to-nothin' and I joined right in. All of a sudden, the chattering going on around me became muffled. I knew something wasn't right. My head felt very full. It was as though I could hear them, but couldn't make sense of what they were saying, and certainly could not respond. I didn't want anyone to know what was going on, especially since I had no idea what was happening myself! A few minutes passed and I could feel the heaviness lift. A friend sitting next to me asked me a question. I responded. But I could tell my speech was slurred. She said, "Kim, are you alright?" "Yes, I think I'm just tired." *OK, I'm a nurse, for cryin' out loud! I know something's not right!* But, just like any good nurse would be, I was in complete denial.

As we sat listening to the speaker for the morning, I began to feel like myself again. *OK, good. All is good.* The speaker was great and I was glad I came. As the morning continued and I sat listening intently, I suddenly felt a strange sensation come over the right side of my face. It was numb. My right eye felt very heavy and that side of my face felt as though it were drawn downward. *Oh my goodness. This is not happening.* My right leg began to tingle, followed by my right arm. So, just like any good ER nurse would do, I began to do a stroke assessment on myself! *Grips? OK, my right hand is definitely weaker. Sensation?* I scratched my face on both sides. *Oh boy. I can barely feel the right side of my face. Facial droop?* I smiled and tried to determine if I could assess symmetry. The right side of my mouth quivered uncontrollably. *What do I do?? I don't want to cause any attention! I will wait until the speaker's done and then I'll stand and make sure I can walk and then I'll get to my room as fast as possible. I need to look in a mirror. I need a mirror. I need to see what my face looks like.* Sounded like good reasoning to me. So I waited. And I waited. About 30 minutes later, she finished. I stood. My right leg was definitely weaker than my left, but I could walk. I didn't speak to anyone, but headed straight for my room. When I got there, I looked in the mirror. My heart sank at what I saw. The right side of my mouth was drooped and my right eye sat lower than the left. I knew that I had to get help. I knew I was having a stroke.

The hormones gotta go!

I spent the next four days in the hospital, suffering from Transient Ischemic Strokes (TIAs) or mini strokes. The elevated estrogen levels had caused multiple small blood clots to form that were creating temporary blockages in my brain blood flow. I was immediately placed on anticoagulants and my estrogen patch was removed. I left the hospital feeling extremely fortunate that the strokes had left no permanent effects, but couldn't help wonder if and when it might happen again.

Darkness

My son, Luke would be turning 16 in a few days and we were planning a party to be held on Saturday. It was Thursday and I was determined that the previous days' events would not prevent us from celebrating Luke's special day in style. I felt great. Actually, better than I had in months. By the next day, the plans were in place and as I sat on the couch to finalize the last details, something took place that is difficult to put into words. The best way to describe it is that it was as though a huge black cloud hovered over my mind and my body and in a matter of minutes, my world went dark. I had never felt anything like it in my life. *Is this depression? Does it just come and plop itself down in an instant? And to this degree???*

That day was the first of many over the next three weeks, each one taking me deeper into a clinical depression that I never dreamed I would experience personally. I went to see Dr. Williams and he increased the antidepressant that he had placed me on several weeks before, "just in case." He was not surprised to see the emotional changes that had occurred in a short period of time. When I left his office that day, he told me, "It will get better, Kim." It didn't. It worsened.

Being an instructor of nursing left me no time to be depressed. I had a new job at a local university and I wanted to be the best at what I did. I pushed through the day, interacting with the students and the other teachers, never cluing them in on the hell raging inside of my mind. I certainly wasn't myself, but being new to the faculty, they didn't really know me. So I did my best to smile, to laugh, and to teach with some amount of normalcy. *Hmmm... normal. Seems like a very long time ago since that word even remotely applied to my life.* After pushing through the day, the moment I got into my car, I fell apart. I usually cried all the way home. This went on for several days, each day becoming harder and harder. I knew I was getting worse. One day as I was making that trek home, a thought came to me that was very foreign. *Maybe I'll get hit by a semi truck. In my little bitty car, I'd never come out alive. Just maybe.* Over the next several days, that foreign way of thinking became more frequent, and even worse, more comfortable.

After a week, I found it difficult to get out of bed, so I chose not to. Few knew just how depressed I was. I mean, after all, who would get this? Several friends certainly tried. I was blessed to have such a great support system. On October 19, 2009, I wrote in my journal:

> **After pushing through the day, I headed home and I knew I was on a spiral headed downward. I held on until Mark and the boys left for the evening. I got in the shower and I hit rock bottom. I got out and called Kristi. She was at one of her boy's ballgames, but left immediately and came and got me. She held me. She cried with me. She prayed with me. I needed someone to understand the pain I was in. Thank you, Jesus, for giving me comfort tonight.**

Sweet support

As the days progressed, so did my need to make the pain stop. How could a woman that trusted her God more than anything in the world feel absolutely no hope? What could have possibly taken place in my brain, in my spirit, to feel so alone in a world where I was so loved? Speaking of those that loved me...my sweet family. Mark was at a loss. He was living with a woman that he no longer recognized. My boys were quiet around me. The mom that was loud and ornery only months before had changed before their eyes. My 18 year-old daughter, Sara, cried for me. Her sweet heart broke as she watched her biggest fan sink into silence. She felt as though her mom was drowning and there was nothing she could do to save me. They all wrapped their arms around me in love. They spoke kind words. They prayed with me. They were there. Would it be enough?

> Journal entry, October 25, 2009:
> **A rough weekend. I catered a wedding Saturday evening. I haven't been sleeping well at all, so it was extra exhausting. I woke up this morning and my spirit was heavy. I knew I was in trouble. We were going to go to the late service and I was trying to put make-up on and couldn't do it. I couldn't stop crying. I immediately texted my friends and asked them to pray. I know they did, but I continually got worse. Mark stayed home with me and sent the boys to church. When he went to get Logan, I hit rock bottom again. I went to my bed and laid in a dark room. I sunk further and further. I went through my mind over and over again how I could end my life without destroying others. I went through every scenario. All I**

wanted was a way out of the pain. I thought of tomorrow and my heart sunk. I thought of the week ahead. I can't do this. There has to be a way out. I was numb and confused. *God where are you?* **My phone rang. It was Brenda. She prayed with me. Boy did she pray. I cried tears of pain like I haven't in a while. When we got off the phone, she texted me scriptures. I read them. The load began to lighten. A small glimmer of light began to shine through the darkness that surrounded me the entire day. At 3pm, I came out of my room and sat with Mark and Logan. My spirits began to lift. The Lord had touched me. Once again, He was faithful.**

Slipping away

I got up the next day and knew I needed more help. I contacted Dr. Williams' office and made an appointment to go see him later that day. A friend called to check on me and I told her that I would be going to the doctor. She contacted Mark and told him he needed to go with me. My friends were beginning to clue in on just how bad I was getting. Mark, however, was still in denial. It must be very hard on a man to come to a realization that your wife is so very ill. Mentally ill. He called me and asked if he could go with me. "No, I'll be fine. You don't need to go." I didn't want Mark to go with me. I was afraid the doctor would ask me if I was suicidal. I knew I could talk my way out of it if I were alone. He insisted on going.

Dr. Williams didn't ask me if I was suicidal that day. In fact, he never asked me that question. He simply increased my antidepressant. I asked him if he would draw my hormone levels. "No, that won't be necessary. I know what's happening." The normally sassy nurse in me didn't bat an eye to his response. I went home to a dark room and crawled into bed. Later that night, I wrote in my journal:

> **Today was a tough day. I'm having more and more trouble focusing. I am sinking fast. I feel paralyzed. Tonight, Logan just watched me. He knows I'm not right. I curled up next to him and he loved on me. Later I felt it settle over me. Mark held me. He fixed me dinner, I took a shower and then I fell apart. I'm scared. My mind has been consumed all day with how I can take my life and hurt my family and friends the least. My brain feels so different. I can't think logically. I don't think I have good judgment right now. God help me. Lay me on people's hearts that can help me. I find it so hard to ask at this point. It must be disgusting to see me this way. Mark cried with me last night. I think he's scared, and quite honestly, for good reason. I don't trust myself right now. God help me.**

A plan

I walked around the house to various places where medications were kept and began to gather them, placing them in a small satchel. I found numerous narcotics that were not taken following my hysterectomy and a full bottle of pain pills that Mark had been given for an outpatient procedure. I added antianxiety medications and sleeping pills to the bag. In addition to the pills, I had a prescription for another sixty antianxiety meds. It was no longer a question of 'if' I would be taking the pills, but 'when'. The irony? Those that know me best know that I absolutely hate taking pills! But that never crossed my mind that day. I only knew that when I chose to take the pills, it wouldn't be for attention, it wouldn't be a 'cry' for help. As an ER nurse, I know what is done to an overdose patient. No, there would be no ER involved. I would have plenty to do the job right. Very methodical, I felt no emotion. Perhaps even a small sense of relief. Would my overwhelmed mind finally find peace?

Rest in the midst

A friend called me and said, "Kim, some of us are worried about you. We feel that someone should be with you at all times." It was Wednesday and I was in bed....again. As needy as I already felt, this was the last thing I wanted. She prayed with me over the phone and laid me in my Savior's arms. I promised her that I would call a friend that lived closer and I did. My sweet friend, Karie came over and found me in a dark room, lying in bed. I was embarrassed. I was ashamed. But I was also helpless. She stayed for a while and prayed with me. As lonely and confused as my mind would ever get, I always felt like I was cradled in the arms of my Lord. Then why did I feel the hopelessness of depression? I don't have the answer to that. All I know is that my Jesus gave me peace that day right in the midst of my raging storm. That storm would soon rage out of control.

Intervention

"There are going to be a number of your friends gathering together tonight to pray for you," read the text from Lynnlee. It was Thursday and it came at a moment when I struggled to climb out of the pit. It was the same pit I was in yesterday and the day before that. The only difference? It was deeper every day, it was colder, and it was lonelier. You see, that's the deal with depression. You can be surrounded, literally inundated with people that love and care about you and yet be sitting smack dab in the loneliest place in your life. It helped to know people were praying. I so believe in the power of prayer. I had experienced it many times in my life. I'd seen the hand of God move in miraculous ways. But, I must say, it felt like my God had turned His head the past several days. *I don't feel You, God, but I know You. I don't see Your hand moving, but I trust Your heart.* He was calling others to intervene on my behalf. "Praying," read the text from a friend in Colorado. Kim called and left a message, "I'm praying for you today." "Praying for you today," from Marla. Kristi T. texted, "you are not alone, Kim, He is with you." Brenda called and prayed with me over the phone. Later that evening, I wrote in my journal:

> **I need prayer support and that's exactly what You're giving me. Lord, please be with my friends as they gather to pray for me tonight. Thank You, Father, for my friends. I love and believe in them. Please don't let them stop believing in me. I just can't make sense of what's happening in my mind. I know I am different. I can't wrap my mind around anything. I feel like I've lost touch with reality. As strange as this may seem, I know You are with me. I don't feel You, but I know You haven't left me. You've never left me. Although this makes no sense to me, don't stop what You're doing until Your purpose is complete. You are God. Be God. Be Lord.**

Be my Savior. I need a Savior.

Almost Over

Journal entry, Friday, October 30th:
Been a rough day. Mark took me out to dinner. It was good to be with him. I couldn't ask for a better husband. But how long can he do this? Please God, don't let him give up on me. I love that man. After we got home, I went to coffee with Karie. I was very honest with her and she was with me, as well. She told me that she doesn't have peace that I won't hurt myself. Oh God, I must say, I long for this to end sooner than later. I don't want to take the easy way out, yet between my brain and my hormones, I am just screaming inside! I feel so alone, although I know I have so many walking this path with me. I long to be held by a mother's arms. Mmmm, I need my mom. It will be over soon. Soon I'll be looking into my Savior's eyes and it will be ok. Soon.

Soon was here...

"For I know the thoughts that I think toward you, says the Lord, thoughts of peace and not of evil, to give you a future and a hope. Then you will call upon Me and go and pray to Me and I will listen to you. And you will seek Me and find Me, when you search for Me with all of your heart. I will be found by you, says the Lord, and I bring you back from captivity." Jer.29:11-14

Saturday, October 31, 2009. A day, although many pieces are missing from my mind, will never be forgotten. It is a day that changed my life and those in my life forever. I would later learn that it was a day that my hormone levels would crash. If you remember, two months earlier, I was told that my hormone levels were at an astonishing level of 1000 (100 times normal). A few weeks later, after suffering from several 'mini' strokes, the neurologists stopped my estrogen therapy, causing me to go into what would be called 'estrogen withdrawal'. The estrogen levels in my bloodstream plummeted from 1000 to zero in a matter of days and I crashed.....hard.

I woke up intending to go kayaking with a friend, Lisa. She knew I had been suffering and graciously offered to take me out on the lake for a day of relaxation. The weather was perfect. It was a sunny, beautiful day. I began to get ready and I began to feel my spirits sink. *Why??? I was about to go spend the day with a wonderful friend. Why would I feel this way?* Mark sensed what I was feeling. I cried and told him that I wasn't sure I could do it. He said, "Go Kim, it will do you good to get out of the house and be with Lisa." And it did. I needed a break from what was going on in my mind and that's exactly what I got. The water was calm and so were my spirits. It was good to be with a precious friend that was okay with my silence. *Thank You, Lord. This is just what I needed.*

My ride home was short. In fact, only about five minutes. But, that's all it took. By the time I reached home, I hit bottom. I was confused and frustrated. *Lord, please don't let me go down again.* Mark met me at the door. *I can't keep doing this to him. He deserves more.*

Numb and Numb-er

'Trunk or treat', a day of Halloween fun at my church would start soon. Although I had intended to go and help with the concessions, I knew I wasn't up for it. Lynnlee called. "My son is wheezing and coughing and I'm not sure if I should take him to the ER or not. Can you bring your stethoscope and listen to his chest and tell me what you think?" I couldn't tell her that my pit of despair would prevent me from doing that. She was becoming familiar with that pit. She had organized the prayer time for me less than 48 hours earlier. I would go. Mark would take Logan and I, drop us off, and stay by the phone, ready to pick me up when needed. I had always been able to 'push through' when in the presence of people. Most had no idea of the battle raging within me. That's the way I wanted it. A dear friend, Terri, had told me just the day before, "Kim, I've known you for over 30 years. I've never seen you down, ever...not even once."

As I walked around the festivities, I felt different. I felt numb. I couldn't even force a smile, not tonight. I saw several of the precious friends that had gathered to pray for me. They loved on me. They encouraged me. *Oh how I appreciate these precious women of God. They have lifted me up, laid me at the feet of Jesus. They believed in me at a time when I no longer believed in myself.* But even as their warm arms embraced me, as their kind words filled my ears, I was numb. I walked into the worship center. It was dimly lit. It was quiet. My eyes went to a cross that was at a 'prayer station'. I made my way to the cross. A calm came over me. I would be with my Lord soon.

The darkest hour

"Fear not, for I have redeemed you. I have called you by your name, you are Mine. When you pass through the waters, I will be with you. And through the rivers, they shall not overflow you. When you walk through the fire, you shall not be burned, nor shall the flame scorch you. For I am the Lord your God, the Holy One of Israel, your Savior." Is. 43: 1-3

At some point during the previous hour, my mind completely 'snapped'. I lost touch with all reality. Some of what happened over the next six hours, I remember very clearly. Other pieces of the story were told to me by those involved that night.

I called Mark and asked him to come and get me. I found a friend, Rhonda, and asked her to see that Logan got home. I told Logan goodbye, never grasping the reality that it would be the last time that I would see my youngest son. I was calm.

The ride home was quiet. Mark stopped and got me a hamburger, as I hadn't eaten all day. In fact, I had eaten very little over the last three weeks. My frail, weak body was proof of that fact. As we arrived home, I looked at Mark and said, "Mark, will you trust me to go for a ride by myself? I want to go to the lake, eat my hamburger, and think for a little bit." He thought about it for a minute. "Ok, Kim, I'll trust you. But I'll need you to call or text me every few minutes to give me peace of mind that you're okay." I agreed. As I pulled away from the house, there was no sense of grief, no guilt, and there was no fear. In fact, there was very little emotion that I felt at that moment. I wasn't crying out to God to save me from myself. I laid the hamburger in the seat next to me. I wouldn't be eating it.

There were well over 100 pills in the satchel that had been sitting in my purse for several days now. I knew it would take a lot to do what I intended, so I took the prescription and dropped it off at the pharmacy. Another sixty. I was told it would take 30 minutes. I left the drive-through and pulled into a bank parking lot across the street. I sat and waited in the dark. It was 7:45pm.

There were no suicide notes being written, no heartfelt farewells to my family and friends. My broken mind didn't even think to do those things. My family would have no real answers. They would never know what had gone so very wrong with the woman they knew as strong and loving. Would they understand that this had nothing to do with them? Would they always wonder what they might have done differently to change the outcome? Those were not questions that my mind was pondering. I wasn't questioning. I wasn't planning. I just sat in the dark parking lot and stared. I didn't hear my phone signaling a text message. Nor did I hear the next, nor the next. What my sick mind didn't know at the time was that numerous text messages were coming from friends and family members, randomly texting me. Much later I would learn that those texts relayed messages of intercession on my behalf, moments before I would be taking my own life. Some texts were from out of state, others from people that I hadn't seen or spoken with in months, stating that they had no idea why, but that they felt an urgency to pray for me. I also was unaware of the circle of prayer that was taking place in a parking lot several miles away on my behalf. They knew something was happening and I would be told later that it was as though 'heaven came down on us as we prayed'. Wow. At the *precise moment* I needed prayer, He called upon His people to intercede for me!

Salvation

I don't remember making the decision to call her. It wasn't to ask for help. This friend and I had experienced 'life' together during our three-year friendship. It was incredibly special, but my insecurities had damaged the friendship. Did I call her out of desperation? I have no idea. What I do know is that the Lord most likely used that call to save my life. I don't remember having an agenda. I'm not certain of what I said, but she realized pretty quickly that I was in trouble. I didn't know Mark had tried to call numerous times in the few minutes I was on the phone with her. It was enough to clue him in. He found the empty pill bottles. When he called again, I answered. I wanted to simply tell him how sorry I was, that I loved him and that this had nothing to do with him, but that I had no choice. His voice was loud with anger and panic. It had now been 40 minutes since I left the house. "What are you doing, Kim?!" "Where are you?!" I refused to tell him. He said he was going to call 911. Fear overtook me. My sick mind envisioned the police knowing my car, finding me, and I would be alone. All alone. The very thought panicked me. "Don't call 911!!!" "Then you come home right now!" He said, "You've got ten minutes to be home or I'm calling 911!" "Ok, I'm coming home." I hung up the phone and drove through the pharmacy to pick up the medication I was waiting for. I had no intention of going home. But I also had no intention of being found... alive.

As I pulled away from the pharmacy with the pills sitting in my lap, my sick mind raced. *I can't be on a public street. They will know my car.* I pulled into a nearby neighborhood. I pulled into a driveway. It was quiet and dark. No cars were in the driveway. *No one's home. I can do it here.* I heard noises. People were walking behind the car. Trick or treaters. *Really??* I began to panic. *Where can I go where the police won't find me?? They will know my car! They will take me away and I will be **alone**!* My phone rang. It was Karie. I answered the call, panicked, "Don't let Mark call 911! You have to call him and tell him he can't call 911!!" Karie had been on this journey with me. She knew me well. We were best friends in high school and had kind of fallen out of touch, like old friends do. We got together several months earlier and she sensed that something wasn't quite right. She kept close tabs on me and over the past few weeks, we had become very close. When I answered the phone, she knew by the tone of my voice that the time had come. The night before as we sat at a coffee shop, she came to the realization that I was losing touch with reality. Twenty-four hours earlier, she gathered with several of my friends, praying for wisdom. *Do we force Kim to go to a psych facility, where we know she'll be safe?* They sought the Lord on my behalf. The answer they got? ***Be still and know that I am God.***

Karie calmly replied to my frantic screaming demands, "Kim, tell me where you're at. Have you done anything to hurt yourself?" "I will tell you where I am if you will call Mark and tell him not to call 911! He can't call 911!" He would listen to Karie. He trusted her. He had grown close to all of my friends over the past few weeks. They were a great support to him at a time when he had no clue how to handle this very unfamiliar situation. "I will call Mark, but you have to promise me to answer your phone when I call you back." I promised. Seconds later, she called back. "He won't call 911. Now, where are you?" I drove out of the neighborhood I was in and into an empty parking lot. My mind's ability to sort through any other options froze. I told her of my location.

Sirens

Very little was going through my mind. It felt like only seconds passed when Karie drove up and got into the passenger's seat of my car. A sense of relief came over me. Not because my plan had come to a halt, but because I was not alone. My very sick mind was so fixated on being found by authorities and being alone. I can't really explain that unusual fear of abandonment that gripped me that night, but it was that very fear that the Lord used to stop what was certain to happen, literally within minutes. Moments later, several other friends drove into the parking lot. *What's going on?? How does everyone know I'm here?* Sirens. I heard sirens. I don't remember a lot, but I was told later that I 'lost' it, I freaked out. The last bit of my mind that was holding on for dear life, snapped. Fear overtook me and was displayed in ways that left on-looking friends crying out to the Lord on my behalf. The moments that followed are very blurry to me. There were police cars, fire trucks, an ambulance...and incredibly loud sirens. As frightening as that was, I'm not sure it scared me as much as seeing Mark's face when he drove up and got out of his truck. He was so angry. He was scared to death. But, he was angry. His wife had just put him through a hell that he may never get over. *I had lost my mind. Had I lost my husband too?*

Locked up

My eyes slowly opened. It took me a while to realize why I didn't recognize the white cement walls. My heart sank. The previous hours slowly began to reenter my mind. I remembered being taken from the emergency room and placed into a security vehicle with an officer to be taken to a facility. A psych facility. As I said goodbye to Mark, he was emotionless. He was worn out. They told him that he could not go with me. He was okay with that. I, on the other hand, was not. The ride was quiet and desperately lonely. I wanted to scream with everything in me, *please don't take me away!* But I didn't. I cried the loneliest cry I would ever know.

The soft tears were still flowing when I arrived at the eerily, cold facility. After being strip-searched, every inch of my body inspected, and incessantly questioned, I was taken to my room. I was not allowed to take anything with me. I stepped inside the empty, hollowed out space and looked around. There was nothing on the white, concrete walls, not even a TV. I looked around for a clock. No clock. I asked the nurse what time it was. "It's 3:30am." It was Sunday, November 1st, 2009. "Try to get some sleep," she said as she shut the door. Sleep is something I hadn't done in weeks.

My mind was racing with every emotion possible. I was angry that my plan had not been successful, while feeling an incredible sense of guilt and shame that left me feeling empty. I was numb, yet hypersensitive to everything I saw, everything I touched, and even the smells that lingered in the air. My mind was full of questions, so many pieces of the past few days were missing. One thing, however, was certain. I was alone, very much alone. As far as I knew at that moment, I had lost everything. I lost my dignity. That was a given. Certainly, I lost the respect and trust of so many that I cared deeply for, perhaps even my family. *Oh God, have I lost my family?* I lost my mind and not sure I'd ever get it back. And what of my freedom? *Is this the place I would come to know as home?*

I crumpled onto the hard little bed and curled up into a ball. The tears began to flow. I could barely get the words out. I whispered, *Jesus, my Lord, where are You?!* My voice became louder. I said it again. And again. I began to cry out to my Lord with everything I had. *Is this it, Father? Is this Your perfect will for my life? Why couldn't You just let me go home? I just wanted to be with You. That's all!* Tears were flowing and so were the pleas to my Savior. *Please don't leave me, Father. I'm so scared. I need You. Jesus, I need You!!* I laid in silence. Suddenly, a warmth came over me. I'm certain I felt His breath on my cheek. *"Kim. I love you. You are my child. Do not fear for I am with you. Be not dismayed, for I am your God. I will help you. I will strengthen you. I will uphold you with my righteous right hand."* What had been the single loneliest time in my life became the most intimate time with my Lord, my Savior, my Father. At the end of myself, the absolute end of myself, I closed my eyes and went to sleep.

The morning after

I need to write, I need to journal. Over the past few months, journaling had become my outlet. My mind was not right, but my thoughts seemed to come together when I wrote them down. I remembered a booklet they gave me the night before, a patient guide, a fancy name for *information about the nuthouse.* I opened it up. I could write on this. I could write in the spaces between the lines. I went to the nurses' station and asked for a pencil. It was dull and no longer than about two inches. The reasoning behind that didn't cross my mind at the time. It would later.

> Journal entry, Sunday, November 1st:
> **I can't believe I'm here. I'm in a psych unit. The doors are locked to the outside. I stare at the piece of paper that Robyn gave me with a list of phone numbers on it. She wrote them down in the ER last night when we were told I wouldn't be allowed to have my cell phone with me. I'm in a freaking psych unit! I'm not allowed any personal items. I didn't have any**

place to put my contacts last night, so I wore them to bed. I don't know what time it is. There is no clock. I can't help but wonder how much Mark hates me for what I put him through last night. I wonder what my friends must feel after seeing what used to be a kinda together woman completely lose it right in front of them. I had every intention of ending my life. I had enough pills to do the trick in a matter of minutes. When I heard sirens, I felt myself go crazy inside. I don't think I've ever been that scared. I knew my plan was completely busted. I will look like a fool for the rest of my life, at least to those that were there last night. I just wanted to be with my Lord. I wanted to feel His face against mine. I just wanted peace. But what about my precious children? What must they be feeling? I can't go there right now. What my family and friends must be thinking today. They must be so disappointed. They believed in me, in what I stood for. I've let them down. But worst of all, how disappointed my Lord must be with me. You trusted me with this journey and I blew it. I'm so sorry. So now I'm left with looking at these blank walls and I'm overwhelmed with shame. I wish that I would have succeeded. I would be at peace.

I needed coffee. I went to the nurses' station just a few feet from my room and asked where I might find some coffee. They pointed down the hall. I began to walk to where they had directed me. The tears began to flow. There weren't many people around. *It must be early.* I found the coffee, poured a cup, and went back to my room. *This is surreal. This doesn't happen to 'normal' women.* I remember my pysch clinical rotation in nursing school. I knew I didn't want to be a psych nurse. I didn't know how to talk to crazy people. I felt sorry for them, but didn't want to relate to them. After all, I was *normal*. Hmmm....the walk I just took down that hall told me that I'm anything *but* normal! I had completely lost my mind. I just couldn't grasp any part of that, not right now.

A buncha nuts!

***the names of those that touched my life in the psych facility have been changed for this story to protect their privacy...**

The announcement over the loud speakers startled me. It was so loud. "All residents on the west wing need to report to the dining room for breakfast." I wouldn't be going. I had no appetite for food, nor for socializing. The hallway that was quiet earlier was now filled with voices. I continued to write in my 'journal'. After several minutes, it was quiet again. I heard a knock on the door just before it opened. "Kim, you need to come down the hall for breakfast." She had a very kind voice with an accent of some sort. I love accents. In my normal state of mind, I love to joke around and talk in various accents. Not today. She came beside my bed and took my hand. I immediately began to cry and said, "I would rather not go if that's ok. I would like to just stay in my room." She introduced herself as Juanita. Her big brown eyes looked at me with such compassion. "Please come to the dining room. They keep a record of who doesn't show up for activities. It will only keep you here longer. And it will do you good to be around others." "No, thank you Juanita, but I just can't be around others right now." She looked disappointed and said, "ok, I will bring breakfast to your room so that you can eat. You need to eat." I reluctantly agreed. I couldn't say no to this sweet thing that was trying to reach out to me.

I needed to talk to my friends. I needed to hear their voices. I needed to know they didn't hate me. My mind was replaying every minute that I could remember from the night before. I couldn't believe it really happened. *I lost my mind. How does a christian woman that has everything in life going for her lose her mind? Did my Lord allow it to happen? Did He choose for it to happen?* As I tried to sort it out, it became very clear that my mind was still not right. I was now not only hopeless beyond comprehension, but I was also ashamed, embarrassed, and angry. I would go look for a phone. I wrapped up in a blanket that was on the bed and left the room. I caught a glimpse of myself in the mirror as I was leaving. I looked so old. My face was drawn, my eyes were swollen. *Wow, Kim. You truly are at rock bottom.*

As I walked down the hall, people stared. I kept my head down. I didn't want them to see me cry. I didn't want to talk to anyone. I wasn't interested in making friends, I just wanted to find a phone. A young man, probably around 20 years old, stepped in front of me and put his hand out, "Hi. I'm Jay." I looked at him, stepped around him, and kept walking. I know it was rude. But today, I didn't care.

I got out my list and took the phone out of the carrier on the wall. Ohhhhkay, I wouldn't be going far. The cord was about six inches long. *Hmmm...that's inconvenient.* The reasoning behind that never entered my cluttered mind. I began to go down the list, calling friend after friend. No one answered. *Probably in church, right??* I left them messages, pathetic messages.

A brief visit

It was 1pm, a special time of visitation that the facility only had on Sundays. Otherwise, visitation was only once per day at 6pm. *How in the world am I going to do this? How can I not see my kids? What if no one comes to see me?* The horrible feeling of abandonment came over me. *This wasn't something I brought on myself, was it? Is this really what my Lord had planned for me? This is it??*

Everyone experiences life crises, some worse than others. But shame and dishonor are probably not a part of their story. Terrible heartbreak, perhaps.....but are they left without their dignity? *All I know is that my life will be different from this point on. Others will look at me differently, but I can't blame them for that. Heck, I'm not sure I'll be able to look into a mirror and not be disgusted. But I guess that's the price I pay for trying to end my life. It hurts people. It leaves them scarred. How do I get through this? How can this place possibly help me?*
An announcement over a loud speaker interrupted my thoughts. "Kim B., report to the dining room. You have a visitor." My heart lept. I took off, almost in a sprint, down the hall. Mark was sitting at a table by himself. He looked wiped out. His eyes were swollen and wet. "I only came because I felt like I should, Kim. I wasn't ready to see you." I know Mark was being honest with me, but it killed me to hear those words. He was angry and confused. He'd been lied to and manipulated by the one person he loved and trusted more than anyone else on the planet. It had not been an easy marriage, but after 28 years, we were best friends and closer

than ever. He tried to protect me over the past several weeks and felt like a failure. He was hurt at the core of who he was as a man and as a husband. He didn't stay long and as the doors closed behind him, I was left with the reality that I may have lost him. That was a reality that I could not face. Not now. Not ever.

Unwelcome

I found the phones again and began making calls. As I was talking to a friend, a young, 'rough around the edges' African-American woman approached me and said, "get off the phone, your time is up!" Ok, so to say that it was uncharacteristic of me to reply the way I did would be an understatement, but I was out of my mind, *right*? I yelled, "Get outta here! I'll be off in a minute!" She mumbled something under her breath and left the room. Others were staring and mumbling amongst themselves. I was not making friends fast, but this would not be a place for new friendships. Or so I thought.

As I made my way back to my room, I smelled cigarettes and alcohol and heard the roar of either a train or a snore, not sure which. *Huh oh, wrong room.* I quickly walked out and looked at the hand-written names posted on the door. No, there was my name. But, there was another name written under mine. Just when I thought my day couldn't get any worse, it did. The tears began to flow as I sat on the floor outside my room. I'm not sure, but I think I felt the wall shake with her every breath. *Really, Lord, really?*

A sweet embrace

Dinner came and went. I sat in the dining room but ate nothing. I had no appetite. A younger gal, about 35 years old, came and sat next to me at the table. She introduced herself as Pam. She appeared comfortable in this place. She knew everyone by name. She had a sweet spirit about her. I answered her questions, but had nothing more to offer. She certainly appeared pretty 'normal'. *I wonder what her story is.*

As I walked back to my room, I caught a glimpse of a woman sitting in a wheelchair. She gently grabbed my hand as I walked by her. I stopped and looked at her. She slowly stood up and held her arms out. "I've been waiting to do this all day," she said. She hugged me as though she knew my pain. She held me tightly as I sobbed. I could feel the eyes of those around us, but I didn't care. This was exactly what I needed at this very moment.

> Journal entry, Sunday night, 10pm:
> **I got to see my sister-in-law, Robyn, and a few friends tonight during the visiting hour. It was good to see familiar faces that still love me. It was so difficult to tell them goodbye. I never knew I could feel so lonely. God, get me through this night. And then tomorrow. How do I live through tomorrow? How do I come out of this okay? I am so very alone in this place. Father, I'm so scared.**

A new day

Journal entry, Monday morning, 6am:
I've decided I'm not going to make any phone calls today. It's just me and You, Lord. I can't believe I'm at this place in my life, but I am. God, You are all I have today. Please make Yourself very known to me. I am seeking You. Please allow me to feel the stroke of Your hand. So I lay here in this bed next to a woman that I don't know in the other bed, who sounds as though when she coughs, her lung is going to hit me in the side of the face. Yep, this is rock bottom. The only way is up.

"I've seen thousands of people from all walks of life sitting in the chair that you are in at this moment. I've heard every story in an effort to seek attention, in an effort to get medication. I hear their stories and I filter out the lies and manipulation. But, young lady, you are the real deal. You are as real as they come. I'm going to do whatever it takes to help you." I had waited my turn in one of the many chairs lining the hall outside the psychiatrist's office, wondering what this doctor would say to me. Would he give me some 'happy pills' and dismiss me so that he could get through the long line of patients waiting to be seen? I never dreamed those would be the words I would hear him say. I told him of my hormonal imbalance and what Dr. Williams had told me about the neuron transmitters and their response to the high levels of estrogen. He told me that due to his limited knowledge of hormones, he would contact Dr. Williams immediately. He also told me that he believed that several days ago, a portion of my brain literally shut down. He said that his treatment of choice would be shock therapy, but that this facility no longer allowed it. I think I breathed a sigh of relief at that moment. Instead, he would start me on Ritalin, which would basically accomplish the same thing, 'revving' up the brain, 'jump-starting' it.

The doctor looked directly at me and said, "Kim, are you feeling shame for what happened?" I began to cry and he let me cry for several minutes before he spoke again. "Let me ask you something. Would you feel shame if you had suffered a heart attack Saturday night?" I replied with, "No, but I wouldn't be locked up in a psych ward if I had had a heart attack either!" "You are very sick. You've had no control over what's taken place in your mind over the past several weeks and months. You've had no more control over what's happened in your body than if your heart was failing and you had a massive heart attack. I want you to remember that." I left his office with a glimmer of hope. This man is going to help me. The row of people waiting to be seen had increased in number quite a bit. They watched me as I walked down the hall to my room. Jay caught my eye. He smiled at me. I felt a twinge of guilt for being so rude yesterday.

At 10am, the loudspeaker sounded again. "The west wing patients need to report to the lounge for group." I would be going to group. The psychiatrist made it very clear to me that I would be going. My roommate got out of bed, grunting something as she made her way out of the room. There was a knock on the door. "Come on Kim, it's time for group. I'll show you where it is." It was sweet Juanita. I was a bit curious to see the other patients. I wanted to hear their *crazy* stories.

There were about 15 people sitting in the chairs that outlined the lounge area. I knew this room. This is where the two phones are located. They had been taken off the hook for the meeting. They dangled by their short little cords. The leader of the group welcomed me and introduced himself as Ron. He was in his 40's, outgoing, and knew everyone there by name. I recognized several. I didn't know their names, but had seen their faces in the halls. Except Jay. I knew his name. And there's the sweet lady in the wheelchair. If she told me her name, it escaped me. And then there was my roommate. I don't even know her name. Today, I refer to her as 'well rested'. I listened as each told their stories, many of who were repeat patients. Each account was different. Some cried, some were visibly angry, while others were obviously drugged, slurring their words as they spoke. As I listened, I felt a strange sense of connection come over me. I was no better than any of these people. And at least for now, I was one of them. My heart began to soften.

Ron said, "Kim, can you tell us what got you in this place?" I began to tell my story. I cried. My mind was still foggy, but I told the details as I remembered them. As I spoke, it felt strangely safe. When I finished, I kept my head down. A voice I didn't recognize said, "Wow, thank you for sharing that. I've seen you walk around for the past two days, obviously in pain, and now I understand." He was an older gentleman that had spoken of an unfortunate bout with medication addiction and his battle with depression. After group was over, my roommate came over, hugged me, and said, "My name is Kay. Thank you for sharing. I'm here if you need me." Earlier she told of her struggle with alcohol dependence. She admitted herself. It was tearing her family a part and she genuinely wanted help. Jay walked toward me. He had spoken of his family having him admitted to this place. They said that he was acting 'odd', doing things like burning money and eating leaves. He spoke with such articulation, showing exceptional intelligence. He was soft spoken and oozed with gentleness. As he approached me, I could see his hesitance as he held out his hand. I took his hand in both of mine and said, "I'm Kim." He smiled, "and I'm Jay. It's very nice to meet you, Kim." I knew that an apology wasn't necessary. There was an unspoken understanding between us....between all of us.

Flying High

***"Yet in all things, we are more than conquerors through Him who loved us."* Romans 8:37**

Karie brought me a bible that she got from the Life Church to give to me the night before. I didn't want to have my own bible there, as it was far too precious to me. I couldn't take a chance on something happening to it. I was thankful to have this one today.

After group, they called me to the medication station. I would be taking my regular medications, as well as the newly ordered Ritalin and a hormone patch. It didn't take long for it to kick in. It was a strange sensation I was feeling. My heart raced, I couldn't sit still even for a moment, and the woman that only hours before had absolutely nothing to say to anyone, suddenly couldn't shut up. Let's face it, it was *speed* and it was doing more than 'restarting my engine'! Kay laughed out loud as she lay on the bed and watched me. "I'm sorry, I don't mean to laugh at you, but only a few hours ago, you were lying in your bed or walking around wrapped up in a blanket, having absolutely nothing to say to anyone. And now, well you are pacing the floors and you are talking. Boy, are you talking! I think I like this Kim better. I think." She was not the only one that saw the new Kim in action. I went to lunch and although I didn't eat a bite of food, I think I kept them entertained. Some just blankly stared at me, most likely thinking to themselves, *I'll have what she's having!*

It was strange. As 'high' as I felt, I still felt the sting of depression. If I did sit for any period of time, my mind immediately reviewed the events of the past 72 hours. I was thankful for the brief periods of relief and release from the shame and hopelessness. That afternoon, Susan, one of the nurses, came to find me to give me another Ritalin. She joked and said she was going to give me some cleaning utensils and watch me go to work on the place! I was developing a special bond with the nurses. I always said that I could never be a psych nurse. *Who would want to talk to crazy people all day long?* Well, consider this nurse's perspective changed. These women made all the difference in the world to me. They were so kind and nonjudgmental. They didn't speak down to me. They almost treated me as a peer rather than a patient. It takes a very special person to be a psych nurse, and these nurses were true to their profession. They were special.

Another announcement: "It's activities time! We'll be going outside today. Meet in the lounge area if you would like to go outside." *Mmmm, outside.* I had not seen the light of day or enjoyed the sunshine's warmth since my kayaking trip on Saturday. As we walked outside, I wasn't bothered to see the high fences that surrounded the yard and the small basketball court. I took a deep breath of fresh air. *Thank You, Father. Thank You for this moment right now.* A young black guy, probably around the age of 19, began to play basketball. Soon another joined him. They were good, real good. They knew what they were doing, no doubt about that. I jumped up. "Can I play with you guys?" They looked at each other and smiled, "sure you can." I think it goes without saying that I couldn't even begin to keep up with them, but I do think they were a little surprised that this old white gal could shoot some hoops with them. It was the highlight of my day. I loved every second of it.

It was close to the visiting hour. *I wish I had some makeup to touch up with.* It wasn't allowed. I wondered if Mark would come. And Sara? Although she was 18, I wasn't sure she'd be able to handle seeing me in this place. I had spoken with the boys on the phone earlier in the day. They cried as they told me that they were okay. Luke said, "Mom, don't worry about us. Please just get better so you can come home. We need you." *How would they have ever gotten over the pain of their mother killing herself? And why didn't thoughts of my husband and children keep me from even going down that path?* The doctor's explanation made the most sense: "a portion of your brain literally shut off." No reasoning, no judgment, no guilt, no fear.

The long awaited visiting hour came. Mark and Sara sat at the table in the dining room. It was good to see them. Sara cried and Mark appeared numb. There was so much pain in his eyes. They didn't stay long. They said that there were a number of people that wanted to see me, waiting their turn and they would only allow two at a time. It was bittersweet. I hated for people to see me this way and in this place, but I treasured every minute of being with those that loved me. *They still love me.* As I hugged the last one goodbye while the staff stood by waiting to lock the doors behind them, Mike (one of the techs) said, "I think you're setting records here for the most visitors!" I wasn't interested in setting any records, but I was thankful. I was blessed. I certainly didn't deserve this amount of grace or this amount of love that was being poured out, but it gave me insight to what God's grace can do when it's displayed through others. It's nothing short of amazing!

Clarity

> Journal entry, Wednesday morning:
> **My mind feels different this morning. I think the hormone patch has kicked in. It's almost like I can breathe again.** *Can I really be that dependent on hormones?* **All I know is that I feel better. My roommate is going home this morning. I will miss her. I've had several opportunities to pray with her over the past few days. I think she's going to try Celebrate Recovery. I told her that I would go with her if she wants me to. Father, please help her to stay strong. Help her to lean on You. Use me in anyway You choose over the next days and**

weeks ahead to be Your hands and feet to her. I can't believe how my eyes have been opened to "the other side". There are definitely some *crazies* in here, but for the most part, it's full of people just like me, needing temporary help. I am making some dear friends in this place. I have found the strength to laugh again. They have touched my life. I wish I would have let my friends talk me into coming here a few weeks ago. I feel so safe in this place. *Who knew???*

The depression had lifted and I felt more clarity of mind than I had in weeks. That's a beautiful thing, believe me, but with it came the harsh reality of what had taken place over the past several days and weeks. *Whatever it takes, Lord.........*a previous months' prayer replayed in my mind. The realization of what this illness had cost me became vividly clear. **My dignity.** Priceless, really. No one took it away from me, I handed it over on a silver platter. **Self-respect.** As I look in the mirror, the eyes that look back at me are saturated in shame and I choose to turn away. **My reputation.** Would others *always* see me as an unstable woman that can't be trusted with her emotions? **Relationships.** Perhaps the highest price tag of all. But that's what this illness does. It changes who you are and the change scares people and it hurts people....deeply.

When I met with the doctor, he was amazed at how much different I was. He said, "if I hadn't seen it for myself, I wouldn't have believed it." He told me that he knew the important role that hormones play in women and added, "but this has been very educational for me." He spoke to Mark on the phone while I was sitting in the office and they decided together that although I was incredibly better, I should stay for a couple more days. Mark admitted that he was not ready for me to come home yet. Although that stung a bit, I understood. *I'm not sure I'm ready to go home yet either.*

...and then there was another

She looked familiar. I couldn't quite place her, but I knew I'd seen her face. Either that, or all of us were beginning to look alike! She was my new roommate. She was withdrawn and quiet. I understood. I was there only days before. She came in the middle of the night. I hadn't been asleep long, as it was a late night for me. Several of us stayed up playing dominoes. It felt so good to have some fun and to laugh again with others. One of them was Joe, a 21 year-old young man that was a 'frequent flyer' in this place. He was smart, funny, and very personable. In group, he spoke of his difficulty in keeping a job and having relationships. His diagnosis? Bipolar disorder. He told of the frustration of the ongoing attempt to get his medications adjusted correctly. It was a constant battle. Then there was Cindy, a forty-something year-old gal that was in this place for a second time. It was the anniversary of the death of her husband and her desperate loneliness drove her to a suicide attempt. My heart broke for her as I listened to her story in 'group' earlier. She was searching for peace. I would later have the opportunity to share with her the hope that she could have in Christ. I gave her the bible that Karie brought to me days before and prayed that she would find the peace and comfort that she so desperately needed.

I worked hard throughout the day to make my new roommate feel 'at home'. She's so sad. She cried most of the day, just as I had done my first day in this place. Maybe that's why she responded to me. Perhaps it was obvious that I understood her pain. I prayed that the Lord would use me to touch her with His kindness and gentleness. As the day passed, she began to open up to me. She spoke of her husband's neurological changes and how his sweet nature had turned ugly and violent. Medications did not help and she was forced to leave the man she no longer knew. The loneliness and guilt sent her spiraling into depression. The night before, she told her daughter that she "wanted to die." That's all it took to get her committed to this place. As I found out more about my new roomy, I figured out where I had seen her face. Several years ago, she was a local TV anchor-woman.

I remained amazed that the majority of people in this place are just *normal* people experiencing a tough time in life. We had a connection and as the day went by, we grew to be friends. Not forever friends, but 'we're locked up in a nuthouse together' kind of friends. Pretty special, actually.

> Journal entry, Thursday 9pm:
> **I feel very numb to a lot of things right now. It was good to see so many friends and family tonight and be with them. I know I look so bad. My hair is, well, it's my hair at its finest, no make-up, and I'm sure I've lost a lot of weight since I've been here. The doctor started me on a pill to increase my hunger last night. I've not eaten a thing since I've been here and he's worried about**

me. Well, the pill kicked in at just about dinner time. I almost licked my plate. Then tonight at 'snack time', I ate THREE sandwiches, 2 bananas, 1 bowl of cereal, 2 graham crackers, and 2 containers of ice cream. Yes, indeed, the pill kicked in! This still feels like a dream. The shame is almost unbearable. I lay in this bed and I look at the bare wall in front of me and I still can't believe I'm in this place. I lost my mind! How am I supposed to live with that fact?? Will I ever respect myself again? How do I start over? God, Your voice seems pretty quiet or maybe my shame won't allow me to approach You like I'd like to. I need Your touch right now. I need to know that You've forgiven me. I want to go home, but I'm scared. I'm afraid I'll crash again. I'm afraid I'll let my shame get the best of me. I'm so afraid. But, truth be known, I've been afraid for quite some time. Please help me to rest. Quiet my mind. I just need peace. I don't feel the depression that I had come to know well for several weeks, yet I feel so exposed. I guess I'm disgusted that I allowed myself to become so weak. And even worse? That I allowed others to see me at my weakest.

GOING HOME....*yea????*

I woke up Friday morning with the realization that I would most likely be going home today. Still struggling with what I had done and how it would have an inevitable impact on my relationships, I was feeling a bit uneasy about leaving this place that had become a very safe place for me. I knew I had put so many through hell during the previous days and weeks, and although I knew I didn't deserve their grace, I wasn't sure I'd make it without it. As friends and family came through these doors during that sacred hour each evening, they looked me in the eyes and told me that they refuse to stop believing in me. What a gift. My brother told me with tears in his eyes, "I know you, Kim. This isn't who you are. You've been sick, but you will get through this and I will stay by your side and make sure that happens." No doubt about it, I was blessed to have others in my life that refuse to give up on me. That morning, I wrote in my make-do journal for the last time:

> **Yesterday in group, I shared that I want this whole nightmare of an experience to make me better, not worse. That is my prayer, Father. Do what You want to with this woman. I'm broken like I've never been broken before. I long to heal. I long to grow. I long to be the best I can be. I've made choices over the past few weeks, that although I wasn't in my right mind, I am still responsible for. I have a lot to face in my tomorrow. I will face it with grace. Grace.....that's a great word. Grace.**

Several of my new friends sat outside the doctor's office waiting to hear if I would be going home today. I came out with a smile and they knew. We sat together and talked while the nurses got my paperwork together. That last hour would touch my spirit in an incredible way. Indeed, the Lord had used even *this* place to touch me, to change me. Remember the sweet gal that stood from her wheelchair to give me a much-needed hug? She spent so many of her days in this place, struggling with so many issues in life. She came next to me in the hallway and as she spoke, tears filled her eyes and rolled down her cheeks. "You are my hero, Kim. You were so broken when you came into this place and now you are whole." We cried together and I told her that I would be praying for her and I meant it. I told her that the Lord had used her in my life that first day when she bravely approached this quiet, confused woman that wanted nothing to do with anyone. The Lord had used her sweet touch to extend His hope. As we sat together, I prayed with her. What a privilege. I would never forget her.

The roommate that I had grown to love in such a short time looked at me and said, "I can't believe you're leaving without me!" and laughed. She told me that she's not sure she would've made it through these few days without me. She said, "I don't know God that well, but I know that He placed you in my life and I'm thankful." I was thankful also. So thankful.

I said good-bye to several others that I had grown to adore in such a short time. I would leave that day with a very different perspective. Wonderful people struggle with psychological issues, some stemming from mental illness, others just simply from 'life' and the difficulties that life can bring. As I hugged their necks and walked out those doors to a freedom I had once taken for granted, I knew that I was leaving a world that held a lot of pain; not a place I necessarily wanted to return, but a place I was thankful was part of my journey. A place I would never forget.

I said my good-byes and walked into the lobby. There he was. My rock, my best friend, my husband of 27 years. I was so glad to see the smile on his face. His warm embrace told me he was ready for me to come home. We walked outside and it was unusually warm for November. As we drove out onto the familiar street in my little Mazda Miata with the convertible top down, I became strangely terrified. *Was I ready for this? Was I ready for the uncertainty that my future held?* Not sure, but I was certain of one thing. I would face my future with this man by my side. For today……for now……that's all I needed to know.

The healing begins...

I walked into church two days after I left the nuthouse. Outside of family, I had not laid eyes on anyone yet. It was so strange to walk into that place, having no idea who 'knew'. If I could have looked into their eyes, I might've had a better idea of what they were thinking, but I couldn't do that. I kept my head down. I was warmly embraced by two friends, one of which started crying. It kills me to know how badly I hurt those that love and care about me. For several weeks, they had done everything they knew to do in order to help me. *I let them down.* The thought overwhelmed me. I found myself unable to do anything but cry during the service. *I shouldn't have come, I wasn't ready.* It was prayer time. I sat in my seat, covered my face, and wept. Ok, let's be real here, I bawled like a baby! My sister in law, Robyn, leaned over and said, "Kim, I'm going to go down to the altar and be anointed for you." Words of grace, just when I needed them.

Sweet Momma

There had been so many times over the past weeks and months that I longed for a mother's touch, longed for my mother to cradle me in her arms, to hold me and to cry with me. But, the fact is, my mother doesn't know what's taken place in my life for a few years. She has Alzheimer's. She was diagnosed at a relatively young age, 66. But, to tell you the truth, although I love my mother dearly, our relationship changed drastically long before her illness began. As I started my healing process, my heart began to break in two for my mother as I came to realizations that opened my eyes to truth that I'm not certain I can fully reconcile.

I go to the nursing home frequently to see my mom. The visits are very different after leaving the nuthouse. I look at her with softer eyes. I sit with her, I hold her hand, and I long for the opportunity to speak words that her broken mind could understand. *If only I had known then what I know now.* I long to tell her that I get it; I understand what happened to her; that I'm so sorry that I stopped believing in her; that I fully grasp the shame that follows hurting those you love; that I understand too well the confusion that takes over your mind, causing you to act like you would not normally act, to do things that are out of character for you. I wish I could ask her to forgive me.

She was 48 years old and began to display an uncharacteristic insecurity about her. She seemed to need constant approval from others. Her personality was changing before our eyes. I was in high school and remember vividly telling one of my friends, "I think my mom is going crazy, she must be going through the change!" Over the next year, my mom found the security she was missing in another man's arms. During that time, her strange behavior drove not only her family away, but all of her friends as well. At the end of that year, she found herself divorced, alone, and scared. I became a newlywed the same month that her and my father divorced. She was at our house, almost daily, crying and asking for help. She had lost everything and everyone around her and had no one to blame but herself. She found herself living in a run-down apartment, dating random men from every walk of life. Although I tried not to turn my back on her, she was driving her children further away. We were disgusted at the woman she had seemingly turned into overnight.

Several years went by and my mother lived a life of self-condemnation that was destroying her. She no longer resembled the mother that raised me and taught me the ways of the Lord. My brothers and I met with her and told her that we had forgiven her and told her it was time that she forgave herself. Although I truly believe she wanted to do just that, I don't think the shame of what her life had become would ever allow her that grace.

I have no doubt that at the age of 48 years, my mother was in fact going through 'the change' and that her hormones were completely out of control. I look back now and see a familiar trend of personality changes. The insecurity that my mother displayed is painfully recognizable. *Could it be that all she needed was a little hormone replacement therapy???* Perhaps she needed some professional counseling. She needed her family to refuse to give up on her. She needed her daughter to look her in the eyes and tell her, "This isn't you mom. I know who you are and this isn't you! I believe in you and I'm not leaving you." She needed others to gather around her in prayer and support, rather than leaving her on the battlefield by herself, wounded and dying.

My mom lost everything that was precious to her. She lost her marriage of 25 years, her family (as a unit), every one of her friends, the respect of others, and she lost her dignity. She was battling a hormonal imbalance and no one stayed on the battlefield and fought for her....not even her daughter. Even though she made some very poor choices during her struggle, my heart will forever ache over the fact that I left her to face her consequences alone.

So I look at her, I hold her hand, and I cry. She just grins at me. She has no idea that we have shared the same path, at a different time and at a different place, but we walked the same road. Her sweet, gentle spirit doesn't feel the pain of rejection anymore. She feels no shame. For that I am thankful. *I love you, momma. I love you.*

The story ends, but the healing continues...

Journal entry, 4/25/10
It feels like you've called me to a season of isolation, Lord...isolation with You. I feel alone, but I know You are drawing me closer to You. I know You have given me numerous wonderful friends, but for now, I am to be quiet. I am to seek Your face on a whole different level. And if You choose to lift me to higher places, then praise Your name. I

**will wait for that day. If You choose to leave
me in this place, I will keep my eyes on You
and I will only ask that You keep my spirit
from breaking, keep my heart from
breaking, and purify me, purify my
faith. Make me into the woman You
want me to be. Be God like never before
in this woman's life. Be God.**

Friends often ask me, "Do you feel back to normal yet?" Well, to tell you the truth, I'm not sure what 'normal' feels like anymore. I've been to hell and back. Normal will never look the same.

To say that this has been a humbling experience is such an understatement. The illness of anxiety and/or depression can take a strong, confident woman that lives to be an encourager to those around her and break her into a weak and scared individual that those around her don't even recognize anymore. It can crush the toughest spirit. It can cause a woman surrounded by love to feel completely alone. It can take a woman that attempts to live each moment by faith to feeling completely abandoned by her Lord. But, one thing is for certain. It will change that woman.

Friends tell me that I am different, perhaps a little more distant. Don't get me wrong. I'm still a 'girl's girl', I adore my girlfriends. But this experience did, in fact, change me. I look at life differently. I look at love with more intimacy. I look at emotional and mental illness with more understanding and grace. I enjoy the peace that engulfs my mind and I am strangely satisfied with being still, being quiet. I embrace the gift of laughter…oh, what a gift. I cherish the hugs of those that love me. I am forever changed.

Simply put, *I will live the life that I've been given*…….

Section Two:

Words to my hormonal sister...

Words of Reflection.....
 Words of Encouragement

I pray the Lord use the following pages at just the precise time you need to hear them.

RIGHT WHERE YOU ARE

If you fall into the broad category of 'hormonal', you are suffering from one or more of the symptoms of being hormonal and trust me, there's a bunch of them. I'm convinced there are days when I've suffered from every stinking one of them at one time! There are also varying degrees of these symptoms. The end result? You're not yourself. Let's face it, there are times when others 'tolerate' being around you.....heck, there are times when you tolerate being around yourself! The woman that once had so much control over her emotions is completely out of control. Are there days you feel like you're going crazy? If you've read the previous pages, you know that I skipped all the light hormonal symptoms and went straight to the crazy.

Are you so full of anxiety that you find it difficult to function? Do you find that you're forgetting things or you're smack in the middle of a sentence and completely forget where your thoughts were headed? Or, perhaps you feel the need to 'hang on' to others more than you ever have and you find that others' words or actions (or lack thereof) are much more hurtful than ever before. Hosting an unusual number of pity parties? Do you find that you are struggling to find the joy in life that used to come so naturally for you? Is the carefree woman that everyone loves becoming more and more unfamiliar to you and to those around you? Is getting up and facing the day becoming more and more of a challenge? Is getting a good night's sleep something of the past? Does *not* facing tomorrow almost bring a sense of relief?

At this point, I could say, 'just have more faith' or 'pray more', but I won't because that's not the answer. This struggle is probably not about your spiritual walk. If it seems to be getting worse, it's not because you're not praying enough or you don't have enough faith. This is a physical issue regarding an imbalance of hormonal chemicals that can greatly have an effect on the brain. Unfortunately, others that have not been directly hit by hormones just don't get that. They may see it only as an emotional or mental issue. There indeed may be something going on chemically in your brain, but it may be accentuated tremendously by a hormone imbalance.

Wherever you are emotionally, mentally, and spiritually, He is right there with you. He's not waiting for you to reach a certain point in your walk with Him. No sister, He's so very close at this very moment. Take His hand, right where you're at, take His hand. He's not going to leave you. So just be still and know that He is God. It may feel out of control to you, but He's got this. He adores you. Don't go off in a panic and leave Him. Just be still and know that He is God. You don't have to have answers; you don't have to feel a sense of control; just rest. He's with you.....right where you are.

HELP!

If you think you are hormonal, depressed, full of anxiety, or all of the above, I want to encourage you to seek professional help, if you haven't done so already. Or perhaps you've done so and you aren't feeling any better. Hear me, sister, *find someone that can help you!* I have been in contact with numerous women that have told me that they went to their doctor and they refused to test their hormones, but rather put them on an antidepressant. Don't get me wrong, I'm a believer in antidepressants. But there are statistics that show that the largest group of individuals on antidepressants are women from the ages of 45-55. Don't you find that interesting? *Just* at the precise time of perimenopause and full-blown menopause, women are suffering with emotional issues? The interesting part of that to me is that it seems like a 'no brainer', but so many medical professionals don't *buy into* the hormonal thing. When I began feeling anxiety (that was the first symptom for me...hot flashes were a close second), my doctor started me on antianxiety medications. Next, we tried antidepressants. When none of that worked, my doctor decided to try an estrogen patch. It is *no* exaggeration when I say that within 48 hours, I felt relief. I'm *so* thankful my doctor was willing to try hormone therapy for my emotional issues. However, not all doctors will do so. Find the right doctor for *you*. Don't settle for anyone that won't do whatever it takes to get you feeling better. There are some doctors that specialize in hormones. If needed, find one.

If you are having thoughts of hurting yourself, please

let someone know. Your mind has led you to believe that you have no other choice. The fact is, you *do* have another choice. It may look as though tomorrow is not an option. Let me tell you that tomorrow needs to happen for you. Your Lord has a plan for you and it is to ***give you a future and a hope!*** Jer 29:11. Settle for nothing less. You *will* get through this, one day at a time. I pray this book will give you encouragement as you fight this battle. *Keep fighting!* You *will* win and it will be the sweetest victory you've ever had.

WHERE IS HE???

You may feel as though you are 'stuck'. You look at yesterday and you are in the same spot today. Frustrating, isn't it? It can be paralyzing; the anxiety, the constant sense of depression that seems to loom over you. Take a deep breath. *Be still and know that I am God.* Do you hear that, really hear that? Be still. Period. Let God be God. Perhaps you don't feel Him right now. You are seeking, but you just don't feel Him. You cry out to Him and it feels as though your words are empty. Know this: that feeling is just that, it's a feeling. It's not reality. He's right there, He's not left your side. Trust that. Believe that.

When I'm not teaching, I'm an ER nurse. We get a lot of sick little children and unfortunately we have to do unpleasant things to those babies to help them in their time of need, things like poke them with needles, etc., you get the picture. I watch these little ones looking frantically for their mommy. If they're old enough to talk, they're screaming for them. You can see it in their eyes. *Why is she letting them do this to me? Where did she go??? I need her!* And no matter how many times I tell them, "your mommy is right here, you can't see her, but I promise, she's here." In the background, I hear the sweet mom crying, saying, "I'm here, baby, I'm here." But they don't stop screaming and crying until they see them with their own eyes.

Maybe you can relate to that today. *Where are you, Lord? Why do I feel as though You've left me? Where is the peace that You promise?* Can you just believe that He has not left your side and for right now, for this moment, allow that to be enough? *Be still, child, I'm here. I haven't left you. I'm right here.*

"Be strong and courageous! Do not be afraid and do not panic. For the Lord your God will personally go ahead of you. He will never fail you nor abandon you."
Deuteronomy 31:6

LABELS

Remember Rahab from the Bible? If you don't, she was a prostitute that actually ended up being in the lineage of Christ! Talk about a woman with a *past*! During my time of healing, I became very interested in her, studying her, finding out what it was about her that caused the Lord to choose *her, a prostitute,* to be used for His glory! To say that I related to her would be an understatement. She was a prostitute of the lowest kind. Don't get me wrong, that's not the part I related to ☺, but no matter how much healing took place in my life, I still felt the *looks* of others. Did they *still* see a crazy woman? Did they see me as insecure? Weak? Needy? Truth is, probably not. But even if they did, I couldn't blame them. I mean, for cryin' out loud, I went crazy. I lost my mind. I set out to harm myself.

I think of Rahab and I'm certain she wanted the label *harlot* to go away. I'll bet there were times she wanted to scream out, "but I'm different now, I'm not who I once was!" She was indeed different, her story taking a turn at Jericho. If you remember, the Lord used her to bring that great city down. *He chose her!* She actually ended up being in the lineage of Christ Himself. She was Jesus' great, great (many times over) grandmother! God chose a *harlot* to be in the family of Jesus?? No. He chose a redeemed woman. He chose a woman that was willing to be used, in spite of her past.

Do you have a *label*? *Crazy…. adulteress…. needy…. alcoholic…. unfit mother…. alone…. addict…. obese…. emotionally unstable….or even hormonal?*

Any of those sound painfully familiar? Here's what I've decided about my labels. They don't define *who I am,* but they do tell a great story of redemption and grace, so I will go ahead and keep my *labels*. But my Lord doesn't know me by those labels. He has his own labels for me: *My child, Forgiven, Restored.* The others pale in comparison, don't you think? You may have *labels*, but they don't define who you are. *He* defines who you are. My past? Yes, I have one. But even better, I have a future. Yes indeed, I have a future. And so do you, my friend.

I TRUST YOU, JESUS

"Call upon Me in the day of trouble; I will deliver you, and you shall glorify Me." Psalm 50:15

You face today and you feel no hope. You got through yesterday, but you're not certain how you did it, you just did. And now, another day.

Here's what I would encourage you to do. You don't have to feel anything when you say these words, but say them. "I trust you, Jesus." Ok, now say them again. "I trust you, Jesus." Your mind has been going from this thought to that thought, over and over again. In fact, you may be having a difficult time sitting down and making your mind focus long enough to read this. That's ok. Take some deep breaths and allow your mind to slow down. Don't try to figure out today. Don't go through every possible scenario in your mind. Just for now, let go of the racing thoughts and whisper those words, "I trust you, Jesus." And in a few minutes, whisper them again, *I trust you, Jesus.* He's there. He's right there. Trust Him.

WHERE'S YOUR FOCUS?

"Finally brothers and sisters, whatever is true, whatever is noble, whatever is right, whatever is pure, whatever is lovely, whatever is admirable- if anything is excellent or praiseworthy- think about such things." Philippians 4:8

What do you spend the majority of your day thinking about? Do you think about what you wish you'd have done differently? Does your mind replay yesterday over and over again? Or maybe your thoughts are on today, wondering how you'll get through it, anticipating the escalating anxiety or the spiraling depression. Perhaps your thoughts are on tomorrow, as you play out every scenario possible, counting on the best one to play out.

Decide right now to refocus your thoughts. The Lord wants you to look at Him and trust Him. He wants you to love Him enough to trust Him. He knows about your yesterday. He knows what's happening today. And He certainly knows what's going to take place tomorrow. Nothing takes our Lord by surprise. He's not caught off guard by anything. He will not leave your side.

You deserve rest. Trust in your Savior. You know that He's your Savior, right? He *will* rescue you. He *will* deliver you. It's not possible to have your eyes *fixed* on more than one thing at a time. Choose to fix your eyes on Him today, and get some much-needed rest.

"I will keep my eyes always on the Lord. With Him at my right hand, I will not be shaken." Psalm 16:8

FEELING NEEDY???

Perhaps this word comes to mind for you right now …. *ugghhhhh*. That's a word, right? It is in my dictionary. And it does kinda sum up what you feel when you know you are in a needy state. During my times of need or pain as long as I can remember as an adult, I have always fought the appearance of being needy to others. The last thing in the world I want to be to others is a burden for them to carry. But here's the deal, sister. The fact is, we need each other at times. Call it whatever you want to call it, needy, weak, or vulnerable and as much as we would certainly choose not to be in that state…..ever…..there are times in our lives when we do, in fact, need.

Christ has placed a community of believers around you. It's scary to trust others with that need. But don't place your trust in *them*, place your trust in your Lord. He will use others to help you carry that need. He will be your Savior, *not them,* but He will certainly *use* them as a vessel, as a warrior to fight with you and for you in this battle.

Feeling needy today? I know, uggghhhhh. But, I would encourage you to be transparent with someone that you can trust with that need. Allow them the privilege of being used in this battle that you are in. Allow them the opportunity to reflect the face of Christ that you *so* need to see today.

"Share each other's burdens, and in this way you will fulfill the law of Christ." Galatians 6:2

ALONE

In my story, I told of the single loneliest moment of my life the night I arrived at the psych facility. I think it's worth revisiting here...

It was 3:30am and the nurse closed the door and told me to try to get some sleep. Not too much was certain in my world at that moment, but one thing was absolutely certain... I was alone, very much alone. I crumpled onto the hard little bed and curled up into a ball. The tears began to flow. I could barely get the words out. I whispered, *Jesus, my Lord, where are You?!* My voice became louder. I said it again. And again. I began to cry out to my Lord with everything I had. *Is this it, Father? Is this Your perfect will for my life? Why couldn't You just let me go home? I just wanted to be with You. That's all!* Tears were flowing and so were the pleas to my Savior. *Please don't leave me, Father. I'm so scared. I need You. Jesus, I need You!!* I laid in silence. Suddenly, a warmth came over me. I'm certain I felt His breath on my cheek. "*Kim. I love you. You are my child. Do not fear for I am with you. Be not dismayed, for I am your God. I will help you. I will strengthen you. I will uphold you with my righteous right hand.*" What had been the single loneliest time in my life became the most intimate time with my Lord, my Savior, my Father. At the end of myself, the absolute end of myself, I closed my eyes and went to sleep.

Feeling alone today? You may be surrounded by people that love you and yet, you still feel lonely. Quite frankly, it can be the most desperate feeling you will ever know. Can you believe me if I say, You are not alone? He's right there, I promise. Allow Him to show Himself to you right now.

DO YOU KNOW HIM?

"Now acquaint yourself with Him and be at peace; therefore good will come to you. Receive instruction from His mouth, and lay up His words in your heart."
Job 22:21,22

There are times in life when we are only to be quiet before the Lord and listen. That can be difficult, especially if you're the kind of woman that needs to see results *today*. You are ready to feel like yourself again, move ahead, learn whatever lessons need to be learned, and be done with this season of life. Am I close? But remember, *My thoughts are not your thoughts, and neither are your ways My ways...*

Could He be telling you to just sit still and *acquaint yourself with Him* (love these next few words) and *be at peace*? Listen for His voice, He *will* speak. If you let Him, He will get *so* close to you that you will *feel His breath on your cheek*. Did you get that??? You will feel His breath on your cheek! And one thing is for certain. After you have experienced Him in that way, it will leave you wanting more. You will find that you are spending *more* time sitting quietly before Him, not wanting to miss one precious moment with your Savior. This season of life will begin to look different. You will realize that He is using this time to draw you unto Himself, so close that you come to know Him in ways that you wouldn't have otherwise. You are becoming acquainted with Jesus Christ Himself and the result? *Peace.* Nothing sounds better, does it?

Have a seat. There's someone I want you to get acquainted with.......

LET GO OF YESTERDAY

"Do not remember the former things, nor consider the things of old. Behold I will do a new thing. Now it shall spring forth, shall you not know it? I will even make a road in the wilderness and rivers in the desert."
Isaiah 43:18,19

Do you have a yesterday that at least for a moment makes you cringe? Or is it for longer than a moment that you focus on your yesterday? Do you dwell on it? That's exactly what the enemy wants you to do. I want you to do something kinda corny with me here for a minute. I want you to visualize yourself sitting at His feet. Yep, close enough to smell the leather of His sandals. You look up and He's looking at you. The King of Kings is looking right into your eyes!! *Wow. Look at His eyes!* Never have you seen eyes that reflect so much love. And grace.... mmmmm, you need grace right about now. His tender voice says, *Can you leave yesterday with Me, right here, right now? You've carried it too long. Let me take it from you and show you how I can create good out of what has caused you pain. What I want to do in you, through you, and for you will make the things of yesterday pale in comparison. Will you trust me with it? All of it? Please trust me.*

Leave it, right there, right now. Now walk away from it. He will take care of it. It's not like you could fix it anyway, though you've certainly tried. The fact is, what's done is done, but it's in the past, leave it there. Now, begin walking on the path He has for you. It's called **today**. Your step will be much lighter without that incredibly cumbersome load you were carrying. It may not be easy and trust me, you're gonna want to pick it back up. *One step at a time, sister.* That's all He expects of you right now.

HIS PERFECT WILL?

Are you a woman of Christ that desires to be right within His *perfect* will for your life? I mean, you don't want *one moment* to go by without His hand upon it? Then how does where you are emotionally and/or mentally play into that? When you are in the depths of despair, feeling like you can't go on another day, how can *that* possibly be His perfect and complete will for a life that seeks nothing less?

Several weeks ago, my pastor did a sermon on this very subject. He spoke of the difference between His *perfect* will and His *permissive* will. There's a big difference, yet they work together. I don't know about you, but I don't believe that it's His perfect will to see His sweet child hurting so desperately that tomorrow is not an option. I don't believe that His perfect will include days when the mere act of *functioning* is impossible, when depression and anxiety keeps His child paralyzed. I remember praying, *Lord, how can this be your perfect will for my life? I can't even be used in the state I'm in, I feel paralyzed. This is your ultimate plan for me? Really?*

He's taught me so many things since that dark time in my life. No, I don't believe that season was His *perfect* will for me, His child, but I do believe that He *allowed* it in my life to shape me, to mold me, and to make me into the woman of Christ that He desires me to be. And **that** is His *perfect* will for my life! What He allows into our lives becomes His *permissive* will to achieve His greater purpose! That's kind of tough to swallow when you're in the midst of His permissive will. It's hard to hear that your Lord of Lords, your Savior, is allowing this painful time in your life to continue, but it's true. The good news? He's still in control. His hand is still upon you. He hasn't forgotten you. He didn't leave you. And He won't forsake you. He adores you.

SILENCE

"Let him sit alone and keep silent, because God has laid it on him..." Lamentations 3:28

Do you ever feel like the Lord is calling you just to be quiet? Like, *really just be quiet???* Sometimes, we just need to sit quietly before Him. Oh, did I say *sit*? The next verse says, **"...let him put his mouth in the dust, there may yet be hope." (v. 29)** Get a visual there? I do. All of a sudden, I'm not just being quiet, but I'm *on my face!* Face down, with my mouth in the dust. I only think of one word. Humility. Not *humiliation,* but *humility*. My Lord never calls me to humiliation, but does indeed call me to humble myself before Him.

Let me ask you something. Does the idea of the residue of dust on your mouth *bother* you or *console* you? After all, look at the way that verse ends: **"there may yet be hope."** *Hope.* Do you need hope today? Rest assured, the dust won't just be on your mouth, you'll be covered in it. You'll be a dusty mess. It won't necessarily be pretty, or neat and tidy. Perhaps, not exactly what you planned for. Certainly not the way a woman should be approaching a King's throne, huh? Actually, the dustier, the better. Got grit in your teeth???? *Perfect.*

THE RAGING SEA!

"A great wind arose, and the waves beat into the boat, so that it was already filling. But He was in the stern, asleep on a pillow. And they awoke Him and said to Him, 'Teacher, do you not care that we are perishing?'"
Mark 4:37,38

Let's be honest here, sometimes it feels as though the Lord knows that we are 'perishing', but does nothing about it. We question whether or not He cares. As christian women, that's a very tough place to come to, but at some point in our trials of life, we've all been there. We usually don't stay there, because the reality is, He *does* care. He *does* show up. He *does* intervene. Verse 40 says, **"then He arose and rebuked the wind, and said to the sea, 'Peace, be still'. And the wind ceased and there was a great calm."** He showed up. But, during that storm, the disciples look over and He's *asleep*! They are freaking out...the wind is howling; the boat is rocking out of control, knocking them off of their feet! And then the worst thing that could happen, happens. Water begins to fill the boat! They panic! So, you can just imagine their frustration as Jesus *sleeps* through the whole crazy ordeal! Can't you just visualize them looking at Him and looking at each other, mouthing, *Really????* Finally, they can't take it anymore. They wake Him. "Don't you even care what's happening here????" "We're about to perish and you, well, you're *sleeping*????"

Can you relate to the disciples? Is your storm raging out of control and you are left in a panic, wondering when the Lord's going to intervene and *calm the storm*? As I read this story in the Bible, I can't help but wonder if Jesus had one eye opened the whole time, watching to see how the disciples would react. *Will they trust Me? They know Me, they know Who I am, they know My heart. Come on guys, you've seen My hand at work.* After He calmed the storm, verse 40 says, **"But He said to them, 'Why are you so fearful? How is it that you have no faith?'"** Ouch. Could it be that He just wants us to trust Him? He *will* get us through our storms of life, but He wants us to trust Him *during* the storm, *during* the times when we are literally knocked off our feet, and even when our boat begins to fill with water. Do you trust Him enough to wait for Him? **and the wind ceased..**

VULNERABILITY

"Carry each other's burdens, and so fulfill the law of Christ." Galatians 6:2

We are strong christian women that don't want to look like we don't have enough faith, right??? So, the last thing we want to do is to actually tell someone just how bad we're hurting. *I need to show my faith in God. I just need to claim the verse, **"I can do all things through Christ who strengthens me"** at all times and in every situation! And it's not like I'm physically ill or something. People get that. That doesn't reflect a lack of faith or a lack of prayer. I can't let my christian friends know that I'm desperately lonely.....that I have no hope.....that I'm depressed.....and certainly not that I even consider what it might be like to just 'be done'. I just need to be stronger. I need to pray more. I need to read more books. I will get through this, but I can't share this. It's just too personal.*

It's difficult to share our pain with others. There's something wrong with that statement, but it's true. When it comes to emotional and mental issues, most people don't know how to help, what to do, what to say. It's scary ground. But the fact is, you need others to pray for you during this time. It will be the very key to your healing. Don't put your trust in others, but put your trust in Him. He will use others to lift you up, to love you, and to show His grace in amazing ways!

"I need you." Hard words to say. I know.

SO INSECURE...

"Let the beloved of the Lord rest secure in Him, for He shields them all day long." Deuteronomy 33:12

As I talk to many women concerning the issue of hormones, one common theme continues to surface: *insecurity*. Are you feeling insecure today? Maybe your insecurities are very familiar to you. Perhaps you've struggled with insecurities long before hormones came into the picture. And now? Well, now, it's escalated far beyond your control.

I look back and think on the days when I was so insecure and it leaves me embarrassed at how pathetic I must have appeared to those around me. I clung to others' words and looked for reassurance. I desperately wanted someone with me all the time, someone that would be tender and understanding. My insecurities changed who I once was as a confident, strong woman. I no longer even resembled that woman. I was weak. I was pathetic. Sound painfully familiar???

I want to encourage you not only to give yourself grace, but to extend grace to others as well. You are a different person in their eyes. So, here's what you must do, starting today, starting right now: you must take your eyes off of *them* for your security and look to your Savior. Let Him hold you. Let Him comfort you. Let Him *use* others in your life. I promise that it will feel better if He's using them and you're not.

Allow your insecurities to do you a favor today. Allow all of the negative aspects of insecurity to draw you to

Him. Really. Take that energy you are using trying to figure out what others are thinking, what they are saying, what they *really* feel about you, etc., etc., etc. (exhausting, isn't it???) and just sit with Him quietly, with confidence, knowing that He loves you right where you're at. *Sigh.*

THE TRAP OF SELF-PITY

I have already spoken of *need* and all that entails. But, there's something else that we can easily fall into, hormones or not, when we're dealing with pain, need, anguish, etc. S*elf-pity*.

The enemy has a way of taking a true need and mixing it with a little insecurity, tossing in a touch of sympathy from others and *voila!* a perfect combo for self-pity! You have to purposefully decide to stand against self-pity and refuse to go there. Realize that when you are *there,* your eyes are on yourself, not on your Lord. Decide right now to refocus your gaze. Now, hear me when I say this, *it's OK to be in pain,* but turn your eyes toward Him, lock eyes with your Savior. I promise, it will look and feel a whole lot different.

"Restore to me the joy of your salvation and uphold me with a willing spirit." Psalm 51:12

THE GIFT OF STILLNESS

I have always been the type of person whose mind is going all the time. I'm working out situations, whether work or personal, attending every detail. If I'm stressed, my mind goes from this to that without solving anything.

Since my breakdown, the Lord has been cultivating a new element to my personality. *Stillness*. I can honestly say that I would rather sit at the feet of Jesus and just be still than anything else. *Anything*. Stillness is not the same thing as peace. Stillness is an act of the mind. It is a choice. And the more times I have found myself there, the more comfortable it has become for me. In fact, I prefer to be there. I lose track of time. I don't care who's around me. I don't care who sees me looking this way. I just sit and wait for Him to speak. Even His silence is intimate.

Allow yourself to get to the place where you are content to just wait, sitting at His feet. Believe me, it's worth the wait. When His glimpse focuses on you, you will realize this is exactly where you belong. And you will choose to stay.....and be still.

"Behold, I will extend peace to her like a river."
Isaiah 66:12

TODAY

Depending on where you are in your journey, the statement *today is an incredible gift* may cause you to say "Amen! It is nothing short of a gift!" But, truth is, that statement may cause you to feel that today is anything *but* a gift. In fact, it may be that the moment your eyes opened this morning, realization hit of what heaviness this day would most likely hold. Hardly a gift. And it may be that as the day progresses and evening approaches, you have mixed feelings about going to bed. On one hand, you will finally have peace from the storm that's raged in your mind all day (that is, if you can sleep). But on the other hand, you know that the end of today means that soon another day is coming.

Start your day today with these words, *"Lord, thank you for today. I have no idea what the next hours hold, but I know that You, the God of the Universe, the same God that raised Christ from the dead, wants to take me by the hand and walk with me. No matter where my mind might go today, I'm asking that You not let go of my hand. I give you today. I'm scared, but you know that. I'm anxious, but you know that, too. I'm so tired of doing this, Lord. Please give me rest today. Please show me Your face today. I need to see it."*

Today may look impossible to you, but it's not. Take one breath at a time. Take one step at a time. Let Him be your strength. Rest in Him. You've got this, sister. Choose to live today.

"Wait on the Lord, be of good courage and He shall strengthen your heart. Wait, I say, on the Lord." Ps 27: 14

THE END OF YOURSELF

Are you pretty self-sufficient? A pretty strong gal? Have you always been known as a woman that's got it together? Are you one that wears many hats and wears them all very well? As you read those descriptors, are you thinking, *well, I used to be those things, but certainly not now!*

In today's society, it's kinda the 'in thing' to be 'all things to all people'. It feels good. It makes us feel worthy. *Girl.....you are SO good at juggling a hundred different things at one time! I don't know how you do it, but you are good at ALL of it!* Mmmm, those accolades feel so nice, don't they? They sound painfully familiar to me. Although I was a woman that was seeking Christ with all of my heart, I was also a woman that struggled with pride. I could do *all* things (with Christ, who gives me strength, of course), but *I* could do all things. He began to show me that *I* was in the way. As I sought a deeper walk with my Lord, something happened. I was taken to the end of myself. Now, you'll notice I didn't say, I graciously went to the end of myself. I was *taken* there. Kicking and screaming, I might add. The Lord would be faithful, but the process would be painful.

As I walked the halls of a locked down psych facility, it was painfully clear that I, indeed, could *not* do all things. While dining with the mentally insane, it became obvious that I had arrived, arrived at the very end of myself. I was brought to a place of humility that broke not only my pride, but broke my heart, as well.

I pray that *dying to yourself* won't look like mine did. It was about as ugly as it gets. But, I'm praying that you allow Him to take you to the end of yourself. Allow the Lord to empty *you* of *you* and replace it with Him. Live up to His expectations alone, the world's are exhausting.

"But He said to me, 'My grace is sufficient for you, for my power is made perfect in weakness'. Therefore I will boast all the more gladly about my weaknesses, so that Christ's power may rest on me." 2 Corinthians 12:9

IDOLS

Is there someone in your life that you've placed high upon a pedestal due to what's taking place in your life? Do you hang onto every word they say, hoping to receive a thread of hope? Do you immediately call them or text them when the clouds begin to loom? Do you count on them to *talk you off of that cliff?* Do you long for their physical touch? Perhaps you find yourself relying on the fact that the Lord will use *them* to give you hope instead of relying on Him alone to give you the hope you desperately need and long for?

Hear me here, sister. I'm not saying that we shouldn't allow others to be Christ in our lives when we are hurting. But we must be careful. Before we know it, we can allow someone dear to us to become our idol. God *will absolutely* use others in our lives to bring hope and to bring healing. But, they cannot become the *source* of our hope and of our healing.

Perhaps you are thinking of one right now. You know you are holding them too high. Talk to them about it, pray with them about it. It will be difficult. You've come to rely upon them daily. It may be a friend, it may be a sister, or it may even be your husband. Turn your gaze upward and an incredible thing will happen. You won't have to *give them up* as a support, but He will begin to use them in ways *He* wants to use them in your life. That's the way it should be.

He means it when He says, **"You shall have no other gods before Me." Exodus 20:3** Yep, He means it.

"I'M NOT GOING ANYWHERE"

My friend, Debbie, said that to me at a time I needed to hear it most. It was about three months after my *crazy episode* and I was extremely vulnerable to the feeling of abandonment. I really can't explain it. I was surrounded by people that loved me, yet still felt abandoned. It was a very real feeling and when my friend looked me in the eyes that day and said those words, it covered me like a warm blanket on a cold day.

Need to hear those words today? Perhaps you feel as though you've run everyone off, or maybe you truly have and you walk the remainder of this path alone. Let me refer you to our Savior as He tilts your chin up and looks into your eyes and says, *I'm not going anywhere*. He says, "I will never leave you nor forsake you" and He means it.

Perhaps *abandonment* is a sensitive area for you. It may bring a sense of fear or resentment. Allow those feelings to pull you away from the need for *others* and cause you to listen for His voice. Do you hear Him? *I'm not going anywhere*. Feel that warm blanket covering you?

"He will never leave you nor forsake you."
Deuteronomy 31:6

THERE'S NO CRYING IN MENOPAUSE!

Actually, nothing could be further from the truth! Feeling like that's all you do these days?? I get that, but more importantly, *He* gets that. Our Lord understands our emotions. In fact, I believe that He cries *with* us. He hurts when we hurt. His Word says, "He intercedes for us with such groanings..." He cries *for* us! He sits before the throne of God Himself and cries tears of pure love as He intercedes on our behalf.

Allow your frequent tears to cause you to look deeply into the eyes of your Savior. See them? They're full of compassion, full of grace, and yes, they're *wet*. Go ahead and let the tears flow, sister and know that you won't be shedding them alone.

"For we do not know what we should pray for as we ought, but the Spirit Himself makes intercession for us with groanings which cannot be uttered." Romans 8:26

FEAR

"Fear not, for I am with you. Be not dismayed for I am your God. I will strengthen you. Yes, I will help you. I will uphold you with My righteous right hand." Isaiah 41:10

I recently spoke with a woman that's experiencing frequent episodes of anxiety. She's also experiencing *intense fear*. Her greatest fear for the past year has been going to the grocery store alone. Perhaps you can relate to that, perhaps not. Maybe you are experiencing a different type of fear, fear that seems irrational to others.

I don't have a good physiological explanation for that, although an unbalanced neurological system can cause the mind to go *many* places, most of them undesirable. But one thing I know for certain, the Lord does not want you to be in a state of fear. That doesn't mean this is a spiritual issue. But, I do believe the enemy knows when our minds are weak and he capitalizes on that. Fear is his specialty. Our Lord longs for us not to live in fear. He wants more for us. He wants us to have victory over fear and He's fighting that battle *for* us and *with* us. Can you trust Him enough to fight the battle for you? The victory is yours. Take it.

"Fear not, for I have redeemed you; I have called you by your name. You are mine. When you pass through the waters, I will be with you; and through the rivers, they shall not overflow you. When you walk through the fire, you shall not be burned, nor shall the flame scorch you. For I am the Lord your God, the Holy One of Israel, your Savior." Isaiah 43:1-3

"For you did not receive the spirit of fear, but you received the Spirit of adoption by whom we cry out, 'Abba, Father'." Romans 8:15

WHATEVER IT TAKES...

"Be utterly astounded! For I will work a work in your days, which you would not believe, though it were told you." Habakkuk 1:5

For several years leading up to 2009, my prayer was consistently, "Father, do whatever it takes to make me into the woman of God you want me to be," and I meant it. I truly desired to experience intimacy in Christ like I had never known. I was so hungry.

This was my journal entry as I approached the new year:
12/27/08: As I enter a new year, I pray that 2009 will be one of change; change for me, change for my family. May my world be forever changed because of what you choose to do in my life in 2009. Unleash your power, that my world will be rocked, never to be the same. No more status quo, no more midstream. Take us higher, to new levels of intimacy with You. Choose me, Father.

I don't share this with you this to paint a picture of an oh-so godly woman. I know that for a woman that loves her Lord, this is a very common prayer. Most of us want more out of all of our relationships, including the one with our Lord. BUT, the real question is, if I had known what the days ahead held for me, would I have prayed that prayer with such fervency? Would I have prayed it at all? *"choose me"*.... Hmmmm....

How badly do we want MORE of Jesus? Are we willing to pay any cost, no matter how great? What are we willing to give up to experience Christ in His fullness? What if our sense of loneliness and depression takes us so deeply into the warmth of His arms that we never want to leave? What if losing the respect of others and if giving up our very dignity created a sense of coming to the 'end of ourselves'? And what about those relationships that we treasure, I mean hold so near to our hearts? What if we had to let go of those in order to truly make Him Lord of our lives? Would it be worth it? Fact is, our Lord loves it when we seek His face so intently! He adores us so much that He's willing to take us through whatever it takes to become more intimate with us. The God of the Universe wants to be more intimate with *us*! He wants to be the first name we whisper when we're desperate, He wants to be the first face we look for when we're alone, He wants to be the One we turn to when the pain is unbearable. Let's face it, *He digs us, ladies!*

Let's do things differently, starting today, starting right now. Let's pray the Lord does whatever it takes to draw us incredibly close to Him, to get us off of the path of complacency, to be the wives and mothers we were designed to be. *And then what?* Then we live everyday with anticipation and with trust as we let Him be God. It will be quite a journey.

RESTLESS

"...casting down arguments and every high thing that exalts itself against the knowledge of God, bringing every thought into captivity to the obedience of Christ."
2 Corinthians 10:5

Does it feel as though your mind is constantly racing? Is it going from this thought to that thought? Maybe you're trying to *make sense* of things right now, or perhaps you're attempting to play out scenarios in your head, coming up with the best one in an attempt to find peace. Or maybe you're reliving yesterday, playing and replaying the events in hopes they'll have a 'better outcome'. It may be that the anxiety you are experiencing won't allow your mind to come to a rest.

Good news. You don't have to figure anything out. You don't have to wrestle with your thoughts. Sit before your Creator this day, close your eyes and picture something with me. Imagine you taking each one of those thoughts, yep, every one of them and giving them to Him. Seriously, hand them to Him, each one, until your mind is empty. Now, just look at Him. Look into His eyes. Allow your focus to be on your Savior. And those other thoughts? Don't even *try* to think about them, He's got them. He has freed you from the bondage in which they were holding you. Let *Him* wrestle with them. Allow Him the privilege of untangling your worries and replacing them with peace. You will be tempted to take your restless thoughts back from Him. But there's a reason He refers to them as *anxious thoughts,* they produce anxiety. No matter how many times it takes, *choose* to take your thoughts captive and give them to Him. He'll replace them with peace. Easy choice, huh?

"Be anxious for nothing, but in everything by prayer and supplication, with thanksgiving, let your requests be made known to God, and the peace of God, which surpasses all understanding, will guard your hearts and minds through Jesus Christ." Philippians 4:6,7

LOOK IN THE MIRROR

Go ahead. Look in the mirror. What do you see? Do you see someone that looks like they've aged before your eyes? Do you see a scared little girl? Or are you disgusted at what you see? Maybe you've put on more weight than you care to admit?

Want to know how God sees you? You are His child. He adores you. His word says, **"He rejoices over you with gladness, He will quiet you with His love, and He rejoices over you with singing." Zephaniah 3:17** He is not taken back with what He sees when He looks at you. He *sings* over you, for crying out loud!

My pastor recently spoke these words in one of his sermons: "You need to believe what God says about you, no matter how good it is." Worth repeating. *You need to believe what God says about you, no matter how good it is.* OK, now look into the mirror again. This time, ask Him what He wants you to hear Him say about you. It won't be words of condemnation, nor will it be words of shame. It will be words that will cover you in grace and mercy, words that will bring restoration. Listen closely. Hear Him? And look deeply into the eyes of that woman staring back at you in the mirror. She's gonna be ok. She may look rough around the edges right now, but she's going to be ok.

"Keep my soul and deliver me; let me not be ashamed, for I put my trust in You. Let integrity and uprightness preserve me, for I wait for You." Psalm 25:20,21

SO CLOSE

Not long ago, a friend told me of a quote she heard (although neither of us are certain who said it, but it's good). ***Are you walking close enough to the Lord that when He stops, you bump into Him?*** Isn't that good??

I want to follow Him that closely, don't you? What if He starts leading you down a path that looks terrifying to you? Or perhaps just as frightening, what if the path you are following Him on right now doesn't appear to have *any* detours on it? *But Lord, change is coming, right? I'm not sure I can make it on this path much longer. Detour just ahead, right??? Taking a sharp turn soon to get me off of this painful journey I'm on, correct?* Do you trust Him enough to follow Him, even though you have no idea where the path is headed? Let me ask you another question. Will you follow Him at *any cost*, not willing to take a chance on missing something that He has for you, something that you would have never thought up on your own? Just, *what if* He's whispering to you today, *Please trust me, My child. Follow Me closely and I promise you, it will be worth the wait.*

His Word says, ***"For my thoughts are not your thoughts, nor are your ways, My ways, says the Lord. For as the heavens are higher than the earth, so are My ways higher than your ways, and My thoughts than your thoughts."*** Isaiah 55:8,9

The path you are on today may feel very rugged under your feet. It may be dark. It may be cold or rainy. But keep walking, my friend, and get on up there as close as you can to your Father. Get so close that you kick dust all over the hem of His garment. He loves that.

Protecting Our Children From Our Pain

"We will not hide them from our children, telling to the generation to come see the praises of the Lord, and His strength and His wonderful works which He has done." Psalm 78:4

So how is this season of life affecting your kids? I'm certain that each situation is different and there isn't a clear answer to that question. However, I'm confident of one thing. No matter how many *wounds* they end up with from being so close to the battle, they too can experience the power of God Himself as they watch His power at work in you.

My children were teenagers when I went through my struggle and believe me, they were painfully aware that things were not right with mom. They had a front row seat watching me sink further and further into depression. Trust me, I struggled with that. I experienced guilt, which did nothing to help the depressed state I was in. So what do we do with that? I made every attempt to communicate with them frequently to let them know that I was dealing with emotional issues, but that I would eventually be ok. I asked them for their patience, for their prayers, and for their unconditional love. We prayed together as a family and I allowed them to see my tears, but I also made certain that they observed me laying my pain at His feet. I would also say, be careful not to use them as a sounding board, not to 'dump' on them. You *don't* want to leave them feeling helpless and burdened. As you begin to see the Lord's hand at work, share that with them also. Allow them to personally experience how the Lord answers prayer, bringing hope and restoration in the trials of life. And the scars they may end up with? Simply a reminder of a battle fought for their mom...that was won.

SOMEONE'S PRAYING FOR YOU...PROMISE

You may never even know that someone is praying for you, but I assure you, our God makes certain of it! He will lay you on someone's heart. Some will let you know about that *intercessory moment* and others won't, but know this, sister-He's calling others to pray for you! Isn't that awesome??

This never became more evident than during my hormonal journey. When I look back, I see that the times when I was covered most heavily with intercessory prayer was the week prior to my *breakdown*. My God knew what was about to happen and He was saturating my world with the power of intercessory prayer! If you've read my story, you know that two days prior, I received numerous texts and phone calls telling me that they were praying for me. That night, a group of friends gathered together to pray for me, as they sensed a very troubled time approaching. One day prior to my breakdown, I received a few texts, two of them from old friends in Colorado *who had no idea what was happening to me!* That is God. The very night that I set out to take my own life, as I was sitting in parking lot awaiting my prescription to be filled, I received three different texts telling me that 'they didn't know why, but I was on their heart and mind at that very moment and they were praying'. I didn't hear those texts coming in and would not read them for several days after being released from the psych facility. But as I read them, tears ran down my cheeks, realizing that there was a raging battle occurring on that night, October 31st and He fought for me! His armor? Intercessory prayer.

You may feel very alone at this moment. Know that He is thinking about you, He's watching every move you make, and He knows every thought you have. He's going before the Father on your behalf and pleading for His child and He's calling others to do the same. *You,* my friend, are being prayed for.

"Then the king said to the man of God, 'Intercede with the Lord your God and pray for me that my hand may be restored', so the man of God interceded with the Lord and the king's hand was restored and became as it was before." I Kings 13:6

CRAZY 'BOUT JESUS!

**"Do not remember the former things, nor consider the things of old. Behold, I will do a new thing. Now it shall spring forth; shall you not know it? I will even make a road in the wilderness and rivers in the desert."
Isaiah 43:18,19**

People often ask me how long it took to feel *normal* again. Interesting word, *normal*. To tell you the truth, I'm not certain I will ever feel like I did before my *crazy* season of life. But, I have to tell you that I'm ok with that.

The season that I experienced during my darkest days are not ones that I want to relive, but I can honestly say, they're not ones that I want to forget either. They changed me. They caused me to get to the very end of myself and come to find out, that's exactly where the Lord wanted me. It was then He had my *full* attention. It was then that I spent every waking moment at His feet, longing for His touch, gazing into His eyes.

Do you wish you could be that woman you used to be? Do you long to feel like *yourself* again? I get that. But consider this. You may be changing in ways you don't even see at this moment and those changes may cause you to be ok with saying *goodbye* to that *normal* woman you used to be.

As for me, I guess you could say *normal* looks very different these days. I wouldn't go *back* to what normal looked like before my season of darkness. Turns out, I *adore* spending every waking moment at His feet, gazing into the eyes of my Lord. Do you have to go *crazy* to find that kind of intimacy? Certainly not. But, I do pray that as you come to the end of yourself, you find that you are growing '*crazy*'er' about Jesus! *Normal*'s way overrated!

OUR SWEET CHILDREN

Chances are, if you are menopausal, your children are a little older, perhaps teenagers. *Sorry 'bout that*! It's hard enough to parent teens, but to have hormones on top of that challenge...again, sorry 'bout that! Unfortunately, they may be dealing with their own hormones. Not pretty. As christian mothers, we want our homes to be peaceful and lovely. Well, not so much sometimes, huh? That can bring about a tremendous amount of guilt. As mothers, we carry a lot of unneeded guilt. *Why do we do that???* The fact is, there are many times when our children are growing up (especially during the teenage years) and it's just not a peaceful time with them. In fact, sometimes it's a huge battle! That's not what the Lord wants, but I think because we are a people of human emotions and because we are *hormonal machines*, it happens. The Lord has given me a promise in regard to this issue.

"Then justice will dwell in the wilderness, and righteousness remain in the fruitful field. The work of righteousness will be peace, and the effect of righteousness, quietness and assurance forever. My people will dwell in a peaceful habitation, in secure dwellings, and in quiet resting places, though hail comes down on the forest, and the city is brought low in humiliation." Isaiah 32:16-19

I choose to lay my children at the Lord's feet every day and give Him our home. I give Him our home when it's peaceful and when it's anything but full of peace! And He chooses to be there during both scenarios. Why? Because I invited Him and because He wants to be there. He adores us, even when we don't necessarily paint the picture of the 'perfect christian family' that we'd like to be. Let go of the expectations you have for yourself and for your family. It will free you, I promise.

POOPED!

When we struggle with human affliction, time seems to drag. Moments during the day can seem like never ending hurdles and by noon, we're literally exhausted. It's amazing really, but when I feel good *emotionally* and *mentally*, I can get an incredible amount done in one day! But, during my struggle with anxiety and depression, I felt as though I had accomplished great things if I got dressed. Or even crazier, ventured outside! Others in your life may not get that, they may even get frustrated with you. That's ok. They just want to see the *old* you, the *vibrant* you. Truth is, they are scared and scrambling for answers and feeling their own version of confused and alone.

Maybe you don't struggle getting out of bed, getting dressed for the day, or even going to work and being productive. But, emotionally, you're exhausted. You find that if you keep your mind busy throughout the day, not only does it go by faster, but it keeps you from *sinking*. That may be effective, but it's still exhausting, isn't it?

Does it sound over simplistic for me to say, 'Let Him be your strength'? How about, 'Let Him carry you through today'? Well, sister, it is in fact, that simple. You can't do this in your own strength. Allow your Heavenly Father to carry you. He knows just how tired you are. ***"Come to Me all you who are heavy-laden and I will give you rest." Matthew 11:28*** Rest. Mmmmm.... sounds good, doesn't it?

TAKE THE INITIATIVE

In almost every instance of healing in the Bible, the person had to do something *before* they were healed. In other words, they had to take initiative to be healed. For instance, the man with the withered hand was told by Jesus, **"stretch out your hand" Matthew 12:13**. And as soon as he did, he was healed. Or the woman that had been hemorrhaging for twelve years, she **"touched the hem of Jesus' garment and immediately her flow of blood stopped" Luke 8:44**.

Could it be possible that the Lord is asking you to take the initiative to do something? Are you responding with *I'll do that when I feel better*? or, *the Lord knows how weak I am, He doesn't expect anything from me right now?* You may, in fact, be in such a weak state and the Lord is, indeed, asking others to take initiative on your behalf. But, chances are, He's asking *you* to do something. It may be something as painful as *lifting up your withered hand and stretching it outward* or it may be as simple as *touching the hem of His garment.* I don't know what that looks like for you, but I have a feeling you do. Maybe it's letting go of an unhealthy relationship, perhaps it's being vulnerable with one that you *need* to look strong for, or could it be that you just need to get professional help? Ask Him for the strength you need and the courage you are lacking at this moment. Once you take the initiative that He's directing you to do, you will find that you have power beyond yourself. The Lord will begin to work in ways that will amaze you and you will see the mighty hand of God at work in your life like you never knew possible!

HOW DEEP IS YOUR WELL?

When I think of a well, I think of a deep, dark hole. You look down into it and you can't even visualize the bottom. It seems endless. For us city girls, we don't see many wells anymore and I'm ok with that. They make great pictures when looking at them from a distance, but when you walk right up to them and look down, woe. Deep and dark.

How deep is your "well" of pain today? Do you feel like it's so deep that you can't climb out of it? Are you so deep in darkness that you only get rare glimpses of light coming from above the well? Feel alone down there?

There's another connotation regarding wells that fits so *well* here. That is the *well of living water*. Jesus speaks of this water to the woman at the well in John, chapter 4. He says, **"Whoever drinks of the water that I shall give him will never thirst. The water I shall give him will become in him a fountain of water springing up into everlasting life." v. 14** Did you hear that? So, the very well of despair, of hopelessness, of darkness and depression that feels so deep is the *same well* that our Lord can use to give us a drink of *living water*. And talk about refreshing! Need a drink of *rest*? How about a sip of *peace*? Or a Big Gulp of *hope*? Come out of that well you're in and sit with Him. He's got a drink of living water waiting for you. *Thirsty?*

AT THE FOOT OF THE CROSS

"We were therefore buried with Him through baptism into death His death, so that just as Christ was raised from the dead through the glory of the Father, we too can walk in newness of life." Romans 6:4

During the Easter season, our church does a very unique thing. From Good Friday through Easter Sunday, the church is open 24/7. There is soft music playing, the altars are available for prayer, and staff members 'man' the doors in the wee hours of the night, allowing people to enter the sanctuary and spend time in an environment that is quite sacred. My favorite time to go is Friday night into Saturday morning at about 1am. I am always amazed at how many people are present at that time of the morning, with one motive in mind, to seek Him.

The Easter following my breakdown, I entered the doors and no one else was in sight. There was candlelight, soft music playing and a large wooden cross, displayed next to the altars. It was quite a scene. I was instantly drawn to the foot of that cross. I knelt there. Eventually, my face was on the floor in the carpet. To say that I wept would be an understatement. I sobbed and I cried out to my Heavenly Father, releasing shame and anguish of my recent past. I longed for redemption. I sought restoration. I found both.

There was a lot that I nailed to the cross that night, and that weekend came to represent a time of resurrection for me. He breathed new life into me and I would never be the same. Don't get me wrong, the healing and restoration continues to this day. There are still times when I deal with the shame of my past, but my Lord raised me and gave me new life that Easter season.

Need to sit at the foot of the cross today? Want to bury yesterday and experience new life? Allow Him to raise you up into the woman you were meant to be. You'll never be the same.

"For I will work a work in your days, which you would not believe though it were told to you." Habakkuk 1:5

WHAT HAPPENED TO MY LAUGHTER?

"Restore to me the joy of your salvation and uphold me by your generous Spirit." Psalm 51:12

Laughter used to come so easy. It used to be a part of who you were. You didn't have to consciously think about doing it or try to figure out how long it's been since you did it, it just happened...a lot. And now, well it's different now. You long to be in that place where laughter comes easy. You ache for a time when you can just double over and have a gut-wrenching laugh. Do you remember what it was like to laugh like that? If you are in the depths of depression, you probably don't. That was someone else, right? The fact is, that wasn't someone else my friend, that was you. Perhaps you feel guilty because others miss your laughter too. That's ok, they'll hear it again. You will laugh again and when you do, it will feel different than it's ever felt before. You will begin to savor the moments that bring you to the point of laughter. You will see it for what it is...a gift. But, what of today? What of right now? You don't feel like laughing. It seems all you can do is cry. You vaguely remember the freedom that's found in being happy, really happy. Today, I pray that the Lord restore your joy in Him. It's nothing short of a miracle, really, when you sense joy in the midst of pain. But, that's exactly what He wants for you. He loves it when you smile. And He adores hearing your laughter.

You will get through this. The rain will stop. In the meantime, focus on the arms that are holding you. And when the storm has passed, you will smile again. And the laughter? It *will* return and it will never be more precious.

HOW DO I LOOK?

"...for they loved human praise more than the praise of God." John 12:43

Have you ever noticed that we *really* care how other women see us? Maybe it's physical. *Do we still look good? Do we look younger than we really are? Does this bod look like I've carried three babies??* Why do we care? What does it matter what other ladies are saying to themselves (or..gulp..to other women) as they watch us walk away? Or perhaps it's not our physical image, but rather our spiritual image that leaves us wanting to *impress*. Again, *why do we care?* What is it about chicks that leave us needing *some* degree of approval from other chicks?

Unless you are exceptionally different from other women, we *all* share a quality that none of us are proud of. The degree from which we *indulge* varies, but I think it's safe to say that almost all of us have *some* amount of insecurity. Eww. *Really?* Really. Now, like I said, the degrees of indulgence will vary. And I think it's safe to say that the degree will vary depending on where we are in our spiritual journey, what we're going through, or even our personality type. But, here's one thing that doesn't vary about insecurity. It's about *focus*. Anytime we are feeling even the slightest amount of insecurity, our focus is on ourselves. Here's another statement about insecurity that doesn't vary: it does not produce peace. It will cause a restlessness within our spirits that is not productive....at all. Ladies, if our focus is on ourselves, it's not on Christ.

Need to refocus? Does any part of your security

depend on what others think of you? Look into His eyes today and let Him free you of the bondage that even the slightest insecurities can produce. And be at peace.

TOTAL SURRENDER

"Then Jesus said to His disciples, Whoever wants to be my disciple must deny themselves and take up their cross and follow me." Matthew 16:24

Are you holding onto something today? Maybe it's an unhealthy relationship, a memory of your past, an unquenchable desire, or shame. Whatever it is, He wants it. He wants all of it. He wants you to come before Him, bring that *thing,* or that *person, situation,* or *pain* and leave it at His feet. Until you do, you will be in bondage to it. It will be like a weight tied around your feet, preventing you from moving forward.

Can you leave it with Him today? Every bit of it? You may have to leave it again tomorrow, and maybe the next day. But don't be discouraged, it's not that He's not taking it, it's that you keep picking it back up. Even though you don't want it, you have a need to carry it around with you. Leave it with your Savior and trust Him with it. It will be freeing, I promise.

I'M SICK OF ME!

You know those people that always seem to be in *crisis mode*? Something is *always* wrong. Their names seem to appear on the prayer list every week. Don't get me wrong, the requests are most likely very legitimate, but just *so* frequent. Well, thing is, that's me in this season of life. The only difference between myself and 'those people', is that you won't find my requests on the prayer list for all to see. The way I see it, *I'm sick of me*, so I sure don't want to cause others to be sick of me. I'm pretty sure that's *not* the best way to view this season of life, but I'm just being honest with you. We all deal with seasons of crisis differently. Some will share their crises every time the opportunity arises, others will keep every bit of it to themselves, never opening up to anyone. Most of us fall in between those two extremes. There is not a right or wrong way to deal with those times in our lives. Fact is, we kind of learn as we go.

What has been surprising to me is that I always thought that as I got older, my life would get easier and I could relax and enjoy the fruits of my labor! Truth is, some of that fruit *isn't quite as sweet* as I anticipated. My children are becoming adult children and as they make choices for themselves, whether right or wrong, good or bad, this momma has no control! This has brought about a new view of heartache in parenting. There's also the painful reality that in this stage of life, we face decisions about our own parents' wellbeing or we deal with their deaths.

Bottom line, it's a season of life that can bring crisis, a lot of it. I've had to come to the realization that it's ok to be in crisis. It's a part of life. It's a part of the changes that occur as we proceed through the various stages of this life. It doesn't necessarily change the fact that I get *sick of me*, but I'm learning how to extend grace to myself.

Are you sick of you? Sick of being in crisis? That's ok, cut yourself some slack. Give yourself some grace. He is full of grace and He's pouring it out all over you. Feel it? Savor it. His grace and mercy will get you through this crisis. And the next one. And the next...

NEED SOMETHING BIG?

"Is anything too hard for the Lord? At the appointed time I will return to you, according to the time of life, and Sarah shall have a son." Genesis 18:14

Do you remember what Abraham did when the Lord told him He would give him a son? Not just any son, but a son conceived at the ripe 'ole age of 100 years and bore by Sarah, his wife, a mere 90 years old?? He laughed. The Bible says that he not only laughed, but he *fell on his face* and laughed. I guess I kind of envision the Lord watching him patiently and then calmly saying, "You done?" And then Sarah heard the news and you know what she did? She laughed too. My Bible commentary says that they didn't laugh out of disbelief, but rather out of *consternation*, or 'paralyzing dismay'. In other words, it was more than their human minds could possibly grasp.

Do you need God to do something *big*? Does it seem so big and impossible that if He told you that He would do it for you, it would leave you in a state of *consternation*? The same God that raised Christ from the dead or that placed every star into the sky is the God that knows every detail about you. He knows what your *impossible* is. Have you asked Him to do it? He can, you know. And then be ready to be *consternated*! yes, I'm certain that's not a word, but it should be☺

SHAME

"Keep my soul and deliver me; let me not be ashamed, for I put my trust in You. Let integrity and uprightness preserve me, for I wait for You." Psalm 25:20,21

Have you ever thought about the statement, *shame on you*? If you think about it, it's a horrible thing to say to someone! *On you* denotes that the shame is placed upon you and you must carry it. If you've ever known someone that is experiencing shame in their life, that's exactly what it looks like. They *carry* it. Perhaps that someone is you.

Shame is a powerful tool that the enemy uses against us at various times in our lives. It can keep us staring at our past, preventing us from moving forward. If we're not looking behind us, shame keeps us looking down. We can't look at anyone in the eyes, we're just not worthy. Shame is very destructive to the human spirit. Does yesterday cause you to carry shame today? Perhaps you haven't *done* anything in your past that causes you great shame, but your response to this depression does. Maybe your family and friends have recently seen you in ways that leave you embarrassed, causing you to feel shame. Whatever the reason behind your shame, it is serving only one purpose: *defeat.*

If you have been forgiven of your past, then walk in freedom. If today is causing you shame and embarrassment, leave it at His feet. Continue this journey without the extra 'weight' of shame. Remove it from your back, leave it behind, and walk forward.

ANXIOUS?

"Search me, God, and know my heart; test me and know my anxious thoughts." Psalm 139:23

Anxiety can be paralyzing. It can leave you unable to focus, unable to be productive, and virtually paralyzed. If you struggle with anxiety, *I'm so sorry*! Some forms of anxiety can also include panic attacks, which involve additional physiological manifestations, such as increased heart rate and even chest discomfort. There is usually a sense of doom and/or intense fear with panic attacks, as well. Fortunately, panic attacks are usually very short in duration, lasting only a few minutes. Anxiety, on the other hand, is not.

I wish I could tell you that if you just pray more, the anxiety will go away. Or that if you will just get into the Word, your anxious physiological state will come to a rest. The fact is, this is a chemical imbalance in your brain that is causing anxiety. *But,* I must tell you that prayer and getting into His Word will, in fact, bring you rest. He *will* bring you peace, indescribable peace, right smack in the midst of your anxiety. He can 'calm your storm' right in the midst of its rage. There are medications that can help with anxiety. For myself, estrogen is the ticket. In fact, my physiological alarm that goes off weekly letting me know it's time to change my estrogen patch is the twinge of anxiety that I feel in my chest. For others, antidepressants or antianxiety medications help relieve the symptoms. Take measures to alleviate the symptoms of anxiety. It's not something you have to just live with! And then, finally, allow this 'condition' to draw you closer to His feet. Go to Him for comfort when you feel like you're going to crawl out of your skin. Tell Him how frustrated you are in dealing with it, He understands. He is there for you. Lean on Him. Believe in Him. Find rest.

CONTENT IN THE MIDST OF MISERY

In the New Testament, Paul speaks frequently of the gift of being content, no matter what our circumstances may be. Often, as a Christian woman, I feel guilty for feeling miserable. What is that? Is it because I may appear that I don't have enough faith in my God? Does the state of being *miserable* look weak? I don't know, but this statement sums up exactly what I feel when in fact, I do feel miserable. It's not a state of hopelessness, as my hope is in my Savior, but rather a state of human frailty.

My absolute state of being is not in the word, *misery,* but in the word, *content. That's* where my hope is conveyed. There will, in fact, be times in my life when I am just incredibly miserable. After all, this life can be very tough. It can hit us so hard that it knocks us off of our feet, flat on our face. So how do we find contentment in such a state of misery? It's pretty simple, actually. It happens when our Lord wraps His arms around His daughter and holds her close. The situation may not change for now. It may not change for a while. But you're not alone in the midst of your misery. He's holding you. *Miserable. ahhhh, yes,....but content.*

"I know what it is to be in need, and I know what it is to have plenty. I have learned the secret of being content in any and every situation..." Philippians 4:12

GOOD, BETTER, OR BEST?

Remember when Abraham and Lot were standing on a mountaintop overlooking a vast stretch of land? I'm picturing rolling hills and trees and beauty beyond imagination, at least in one direction. The other may not have looked so promising. Because their people couldn't get along, they decided to part ways. Abraham told Lot to choose which direction he wanted to go. And he wouldn't just *go* in that direction, but he would *own* all of the land in that direction. But wait a minute, it was Abraham's *right* to choose which land would be his. But he gave up his rights and relied on the Lord to choose the direction he would go. He wasn't interested in choosing what appeared to be *better*, he would rely on the Lord to direct his paths and end up with the *best*. Of course, Lot chose the most fertile, most lush, most promising land.

So, what's my point? Are you willing to *give up your rights* to what tomorrow holds? Or are you living in the 'now' and willing to settle for what looks *good*? or even *better*? Waiting on the Lord is one of the hardest disciplines to learn. Trusting Him with our tomorrow can be so difficult. And passing up *good* to wait on His *best*? *But what if He doesn't come through? What if I pass this up and then nothing better comes along? What if this is my 'golden' opportunity and I miss it?? What if this **is** His best and I miss it?*

Be still. If you focus on Him, He will direct your paths. And your tomorrow will be better than you ever thought or imagined to be possible. It certainly ended up that way for Abraham.

Ready for His *best*? It will be worth waiting for, that's what He promises.

"And the Lord said to Abram, after Lot had separated from him: 'Lift your eyes now and look from the place where you are-northward, southward, eastward, and westward; for all the land which you see I give to you and your descendants forever." Genesis 13:14 ......oh, wait a minute, he didn't have any descendants....yet. Yeah, that's another *best* the Lord had in store....:)

PARALYZED?

"And Jesus said to him, 'Get up! Pick up your mat and walk.'" John 5:8

"Somedays I feel like I can not even function"…. "I can't pray for myself"…. "It's all I can do to get up and get dressed, much less accomplish anything"…. "What happened to the energy I used to have?"…. "I can't even ask for help". These are all statements I've heard many times from women who are suffering from depression and/or anxiety. The fact is, anxiety and depression can leave you feeling *paralyzed*, mentally, emotionally, physically, and yes, even spiritually.

The good news? The paralysis won't last. The feeling will come back. But, in the meantime, can I urge you to allow others to assist you during this time of need? That may not look the same for everyone or for every situation. It may mean asking someone to pray for you; perhaps allowing someone to bless you with a meal; it may mean opening your heart to truth spoken or encouragement given; or heaven-forbid, allowing a friend to clean your house. Let's face it, ladies, when we are in a state of paralysis, we need help. It doesn't need to be long-term, but for the here and now, we need someone to be the hands and feet of Jesus.

Allow Him to use others in your life, in your pain, in your situation. After the *feeling* comes back and you're moving on your own, take a glance back and look at those days closely. Chances are, you'll see His handprints and footprints all over those very tough days. And it will prepare you for the day when He calls you to be His hands and feet to another.

THE TRUTH IS….

"Guide me in your truth and teach me, for you are God, my Savior, and my hope is in you all day long." Psalm 25:5

Do your emotions have you going *to and fro?* Literally, you are up and down, every day a new emotion surfacing? I've been caught in that very whirlwind of emotions. Too many times, I'm sorry to say. And then I discovered something. If I *choose* to focus on the **truth** rather than the circumstance, the whirlwind stops. **"Then you will know the truth, and the truth will set you free." John 8:32** When the situation changes and my emotions are longing to *free themselves,* I stop and ask, *what's the truth here?* The truth is, God's hand is in control of my circumstances, no matter how *out of control* they may seem. The truth is, He loves my children even more than I do, when it feels as though they are slipping away. The truth is, my Lord knows my pain and will restore my brokenness. The truth is…. Him. His Word. He is truth. *Choose* to focus on the truth alone.

"I am the way and the truth and the life…" John 14:6

SLEEPY?

"I will lift my eyes to the hills-where does my help come from? My help comes from the Lord, who made heaven and earth. He will not allow your foot to be moved; He who keeps you will not slumber. Behold, He who keeps Israel shall neither slumber nor sleep." Psalm 121:1-4

Do you find yourself dreading going to bed because you know it's going to be a struggle getting to sleep? Okay, *struggle* is such an understatement, isn't it? It's a battle. Your mind becomes your biggest enemy. Perhaps it focuses on the day's events or problems, maybe it chooses to replay the words spoken to others. Physically and emotionally exhausted, you toss and turn, wondering what time it is, how much longer you have until the alarm blares. Sound familiar? If so, I'm sorry. I've struggled with insomnia and it is very painful. The fact is, ladies, we need sleep. Forget the *beauty* that usually precedes that. When you've suffered with a lack of z's, the last thing you care about is what it leaves you looking like.

If this is sounding a bit too familiar, please talk to a physician about giving you something that will help you sleep. There are plenty of issues that can cause insomnia and perimenopause is at the top of that list. If you are also suffering from any type of emotional issue, lack of sleep will *synergize* or "build upon" that issue and cause it to worsen. If you read His word, you will find so many scriptures calling us to *rest*. That's what He wants for you. Rest. It is crucial to your healing. It is necessary, even to function. So do whatever it takes to get some rest. Once you've gone without it, rest is a precious gift. You deserve it, sister. And as you peacefully sleep, know that He is not. He plans your tomorrow. And then He pauses and He watches you sleep. He loves watching you sleep.

...WHILE YOU'RE THERE

As you've probably noticed by now, I speak of *being on my face,* you know, *in the dirt*, a lot. I guess I feel like it's an analogy that describes what I look like *at the end of myself*. It's a place of humility (not humiliation), and a place of surrender. What does that place look like for you? Perhaps it's sitting at the foot of the cross, looking up at your Lord, feeling His pain. Or maybe it's standing naked before Him, completely vulnerable (I've felt that one before....I try not to revisit it, it's just not pretty!) What does coming to *the end of yourself* look like for you?

Whatever that may look like, let Him teach you while He's got you there. Let Him show you truths about you, about your world that you need to know. Let Him use this time to be with you, *really be with you*. He wants intimacy with us, ladies. He wants to get us alone so that we can hear Him. Don't miss it. Because I promise you, once you've experienced that level of intimacy with your Savior, you won't want anything less.

HEAR HIM?

"My sheep hear My voice; I know them and they follow Me." John 10:27

You remember when your children were babies? I know, long time ago, but think back on when they were just tiny babies and you would talk. If they were awake, chances are they would look around until they fixed their gaze upon you. *Ahhh... there you are, I'd know that voice anywhere.*

When you hear a still small voice, would you know it anywhere? Do you recognize it to be His? Are you anticipating what He will say to you or are you too caught up in your own 'stuff' to hear Him? Perhaps your thoughts are going from this to that, planning and manipulating. Makes it pretty difficult to hear Him, doesn't it? That's why He constantly tells us to *be still*. Have you ever tried to talk to someone that's ranting and raving about something? You can't get a word in...you try...and you try again...nope, not gonna happen until they stop and *be still*. Chances are good that the words He has to speak to you will bring you peace. Or direction. Even joy.

Do you know His voice? If not, spend some time with Him. He longs to speak words of truth, encouragement, grace, and redemption into your life. Get to know the sweet tone of His spoken word. It will draw you to Him and you'll want to hear more. Are you listening?

KEEP IT SIMPLE

I'm spending the weekend with a dear friend whose daughter is getting married. My friend's brother, Craig, has Downs Syndrome. He's a year older than I am and to watch him, you'd say his life is full. He has a large family that adores him. He has a minimally task-oriented job that boosts his self-esteem and makes him feel needed. He loves to take walks, he adores going to the grocery store, and he will gladly show you his Elvis-themed bedroom. He doesn't have a lot to say, but when he looks at you, he just smiles and then shyly looks away. He doesn't clamor for attention, he's content to sit next to you and say nothing, and he asks for little.

Craig's life is extraordinarily simple. There's a piece of that life that sounds endearing to me. Why do we have to do so much, be so involved, and wear so many hats to feel that we are *accomplished* in this life? Would we feel like less of a woman if we let go of some of our *mighty* endeavors? Do we find our worth in how others see us?

I wonder how much less stress and anxiety we might experience if our plates were less full. I can tell you by experience that it is freeing. One year ago, I was teaching full-time, nursing part-time, catering part-time, and working toward a PhD (full-time). All of that, while trying to be a mom, wife, friend, etc., etc, etc. I heard those words, "wow, girl....how do you do it all?" frequently, but truth is, I was exhausted. The Lord began to speak to me and tell me to reprioritize. I did just that and today I am a full-time teacher with my summers off (woo-woo!) and do some catering part time. That's it. It leaves me with quality time for my family and friends that I didn't have a year ago. Emotionally, mentally, and physically I feel like a breeze of fresh air has come over me and it feels *good*. Turns out, I don't need others' accolades. I don't need the satisfaction that comes from feeling like I'm a woman of accomplishment. Truth is, I feel better about how I spend my time than I have in years.

Does any of that sound familiar to you? Do you need to give yourself permission to not be *all that*? Seek His understanding and His wisdom. And then be ready to let go.

SINK OR SWIM

There have been times in my past when I feel as though I'm drowning emotionally. If you've ever been there, or you are there presently, you know exactly what I'm talking about. It's as though you are treading water and doing the best you can do to keep from going under, but fatigue sets in and you find yourself gasping for air as you go down. You panic and as you panic, you kick and you flail. You feel yourself becoming exhausted, but you keep fighting to stay afloat. You're not sure how long you can do this. Gasping...gulping...flailing...been there? It's terrifying, isn't it? What brings you to that point? Is it anxiety that builds and builds into sheer panic? Or is it fear of what tomorrow holds and the overwhelming sense of hopelessness that it produces? Or maybe it's the deep depression that has engulfed every fiber of your being and leaves you feeling as though you're suffocating.

Do you remember what you learned to do when you get into a situation where you become too tired to tread water? You learned to float on your back; to bring yourself to a state of calm and lie on your back and allow the water to carry you, to literally hold you up. Can you do that right now? Take a deep breath, stop flailing, stop kicking, stop gasping and allow the very thing that's about to take you under to hold you up. Allow your Savior to turn that which the enemy means to cause you harm into *good*. He can do that, you know? He can cause your pain, your hopelessness, and your shame to become the very things that strengthen you and make you into the woman that Christ intends you to be. Do you believe that?

There's something incredible about the power in a body of water that is about to consume one that is fighting it. And even more incredible is how to overcome its power. It's not to fight it, but to simply stop, relax, and allow it to be the very thing that carries you to safety. Wow. Our Lord can take that which is about to completely engulf us and use it for His greater purpose, for His glory, and for our salvation. Isn't He amazing?

"When you go through deep waters, I will be with you. When you go through rivers of difficulty, you will not drown..." Isaiah 43:2

THE PRIZE OF LIFE

"For I will surely deliver you, and you shall not fall by the sword; but your life shall be as a prize to you, because you have put your trust in Me," says the Lord." Jeremiah 39:18

On October 31, 2009, I came within minutes of taking my own life. If you've read my story, you know that it had nothing to do with being sick and tired of this life, but had to do with a hormonal imbalance that led to a complete neurological breakdown. In my broken state of mind, I was left with one option only: to end my life and spend eternity with my Heavenly Father. There was no contemplating the issue and there was no deliberation. I did not attempt to justify my action, and so no suicide note was written. As I sat in my car with well over 150 pills of potency in my lap, I did not question whether I would die and go to heaven. I loved my Lord more than anything in my life. I lived a Spirit-filled life. You see, this was *not* a spiritual issue. Don't get me wrong, I have no doubt the enemy knew exactly what was taking place and he was working overtime that night to cause pain and destruction. He knew he would not have my soul that night, but the pain that my family and friends would suffer as a result of my suicide would be monumental for him. There was a definite battle going on that night, to a degree that I will never fully comprehend. But, it was not for my soul. It was for my life.

Are you struggling to *live* today? Are you wrestling with the fact that you feel so hopeless, yet you are a praying woman of Christ? You may not be suicidal, or in fact, you may be contemplating taking your own life at this very moment, but in either case, our Lord and Savior is fighting for you. Don't rely on your own strength. Let Him carry you and allow Him to give you *life*. Trust Him to guide you to someone that can help you achieve chemical balance within your mind. Ask others for prayer. Allow Him to carry you through this season, as overwhelming as it feels. He *will* deliver you. He will *not allow you to fall by the sword*. And He will give you the prize of life. And what a prize it will be.

THE BEAUTY OF DYING

"Most assuredly I say to you, unless a grain of wheat falls into the ground and dies, it remains alone, but if it dies, it produces much grain." John 12:24

If you grew up in the church, most likely you've heard the phrase, *dying out to yourself or dying out to your flesh,* more times than you care to. It may or may not have been delivered in a constructive manner, but regardless, let's look at what it might mean to us today as christian women. I've spoken of *coming to the end of myself* quite a bit. Is there a difference between coming to the end of myself and dying out to myself? Could it be that dying to ourselves involves a choice, whereas, coming to the end of ourselves is not something we're standing in line to sign up for!

Today, as I fall at the feet of Jesus, I am like a grain of wheat. I can choose to hold on to what I want or I can *die* to my own desires, my own strength. What happens to a grain of wheat that falls and dies? It reseeds. It grows and it flourishes. It becomes *far* greater than it would on its own. But, it had to die first. It had to lie on the ground as nothing. Then, not only does it reseed and produce a harvest, *it changes the entire landscape*!

So, are you on the ground? Are you holding on to *you* and all that entails? Or are you ready to *die* to yourself and watch what happens to your *landscape*? It will never be more beautiful.

"I GOT YA!"

There are times in our lives when we need others, whether it's for prayer support, a shoulder to cry on, or just an ear to listen. I truly believe that there are certain people the Lord will place into that role *for* you just when you need it the most.

Recently, I experienced a very painful period of time in the area of parenting. As my heart broke, I leaned heavily on my Heavenly Father, but longed for the advice and sensitive discernment of a mother. As you've read, my mother is alive, but has severe Alzheimer's. I didn't ask the Lord to send someone into my painful situation, but He did. A dear friend that became a mother figure stood by me and carried me as though I was her own. She cried out to the Father on behalf of my child as though he belonged to her. She loved me and encouraged me in ways that brought healing to my broken spirit. One Sunday in particular, as she hugged my neck, she whispered, "I got ya." *Mmmm*. It was as if the Lord spoke those precious words Himself. What a gift.

Do you need to hear those three words today? Or maybe there's someone in your life that you need to say them to. They are powerful spoken words, whether they come from the mouth of a precious woman or from your Savior. Hear them and know that you are not alone.

"Every time I think of you, I thank God for you. There's no end to what has happened in you-it's beyond speech, beyond knowledge. The evidence of Christ has been clearly verified in your life." 1 Cor. 1:4-6 (Message)

PERSEVERE

"Because you have kept My command to persevere, I also will keep you from the hour of trial." Revelation 3:10

One of my all-time favorite devotional books is *My Utmost for His Highest* by Oswald Chambers. In it, he states, "Perseverance means more than endurance-more than simply holding on to the end."[1] Perseverance can be about waiting on the Lord to deliver a promise or waiting for Him to deliver you out of a trial. Either way, it's about waiting. Ugghh...waiting. It's one of the hardest things for us to do, isn't it? But, what did Oswald mean when he said that it's "more than simply holding on to the end?" Well, he went on to say, "Entrust yourself to God's hands. Faith is not some weak and pitiful emotion, but is a strong and vigorous confidence built on the fact that God is holy love. And even though you cannot see Him right now and cannot understand what He is doing, you *know Him*."[1]

Are you *holding on,* simply waiting for a situation to be over? Or are you enduring the pain that comes with waiting for a promise to be fulfilled? I have a friend that wants to be a mother more than anything in the world right now. But, she's not just *enduring,* she's *persevering.* She has confidence in her Lord that He is a holy God that desires nothing but His absolute best for her life. So she waits. Easy? Not one bit.

Are you in the middle of a trial that seems to have no end in sight? Do you know Him? Do you trust His heart? Would this painful time of waiting look any different to you if you chose to *persevere* rather than to *endure?* Can you look

to your Savior today and say, *I have no idea what you're doing. To be honest, sometimes it feels like you're not doing anything. But, I know You. You are the God of my salvation. I trust You. You will not fail me, so I will wait on You.*
So we wait....

"Commit your way to the Lord, trust also in Him, and He shall bring it to pass. He shall bring forth your righteousness as the light and your justice as the noonday. Rest in the Lord, and wait patiently for Him."
Psalm 37:3-7

CAN HE TRUST YOU WITH THIS?

About 24 years ago, my husband and I lost a precious child at term. She was stillborn. In the early days of grieving, we received hundreds of cards, sending messages of condolence and encouragement. There was one in particular that I will never forget. In the card, these words were handwritten by a friend: *you two are so faithful to Him that He trusts you with this pain, what a compliment.* It took a while for that to make any sense to me. Did He *cause* this horrific pain just so that we would bring Him glory and honor? No. I don't believe He did, but He trusted that the pain life brought our way would do just that.

Are you giving Him reason to trust you with your pain? Are you honoring His name during this difficult season of life? It doesn't mean you put on a great big fake smile for all to see or say all the *right stuff* that good christian women say, in spite of the fact you feel as though you've been punched in the gut. I believe it means that you maintain integrity in your pain, being careful not to *dishonor* your Lord. I think it may look different for all of us.

I wonder if those life-altering seasons of life would feel any differently at all if we heard Him say, *I trust you with this.* A compliment? Yeah, I think so.

"Let your gentleness be known to all men. The Lord is at hand." Philippians 4:5

THE POWER OF RESTORATION

In my story, I mentioned that on that night, I called a friend. It was the call that most likely saved my life. I also briefly mentioned that my insecurities had driven this friend away. I'm not gonna lie, this part of my story is one of the most painful. Perhaps that's why I don't say more about it, but the fact is, it was very much a part of my story. It's what happens to women that struggle in the depths of the emotional turmoil that accompanies anxiety and depression, whether caused by hormone imbalances or not; they become so desperate in their need that they lean too heavily on those around them. In my opinion, it's one of the ugliest parts of the illness. It's also one of the most tragic. It leaves an adult woman feeling as though she's handed over her dignity, one that she's worked very hard to maintain her entire life. It leaves this confident, independent woman literally clamoring for others' time and attention, hoping to fill the void that the insecurities have created. It also leaves others feeling the effects of a very unhealthy relationship. It leaves them feeling backed in a corner, forced to make some very difficult decisions. Unfortunately, most women that I've spoken with about their emotional pain have relationships that have suffered as a result of their illness. Perhaps you fall into that category as well. I want to offer you some hope.

The same God that can bring healing and restoration to your brokenness emotionally, mentally, and physically, can also bring healing and restoration to broken relationships. But one thing is certain. He will reveal some things about you that you may not be ready to see. He will show you that even in the midst of your deepest pain, He wants you to lean on Him and not on others. He wants you to put your faith in His truth alone, not in the words of others. He wants you to have healthy relationships. So be ready to listen and obey. And then lay that relationship at His feet.

You may be thinking, but if that one truly loves me, they'll stay by my side, they won't leave me in my pain. I know. I had the same thoughts many times. But, here's the deal. We are only human. There are times when we just can't save each other and the fact is, we aren't supposed to save each other.

Picture this with me. A woman is drowning in a pool of water. Can you see her? She's flailing, kicking, screaming, and gasping for air. You see her closest friends nearby, trying to help her. They're throwing her a rope to grab onto, but she's so caught up in panic, she doesn't see it. She's going under. Finally, a few decide to jump in and try to save her, but one by one, she pulls them under too. They try to help, but she's so consumed in her panic, in her sheer fear of drowning, that all she does is harm those that try to help. So, as they come to the surface, where do they go? They quickly swim to the side of the pool. They leave their friend in her desperation. They pant in exhaustion. They cry a desperate cry. They wanted to help, but the reality was, it was just too much. She needed more than they could humanly give. You may be the drowning woman or you may, in fact, be the one who had to leave your friend or family member as she cried out in her desperation. Either is painful.

The friendship between us has been restored. It was

a process of healing that took several years and I would say that process is ongoing. I look at her and I see a friend that was affected by my painful season so personally. I know that she carries some very deep wounds from my illness and even though I know they're there, she doesn't reveal them. She's covered them in grace. When I look at her, I see a woman that believes in me, and celebrates a friendship with me, refined and renewed.

Can you allow those that you love to 'swim to the side'? ...to 'catch their breath'? ...even to leave you in your time of need? I would encourage you to do just that. Extend them the grace to be human. It doesn't mean they don't care. It doesn't mean they don't love you. But it may mean that they just can't help you. It hurts, I know. Allow the Healer to first of all, restore your mind and your emotions. Then offer Him those broken relationships, wounded from the battle, and ask Him to restore, to heal, and to mend. And then trust Him with the result. The brokenness of the relationship may not ever heal, but you will. The friendship may never be restored, but you will be. The regrets will soon be covered in grace and you, my friend, you will be a woman forever changed.

A TRIBUTE TO GALEN....

If you read my blog, you may have also read the comments that readers made. Most of the comments were made anonymously, but there was one lengthy comment from chapter 8 from Galen. Galen was a friend of many years. He spoke of how he related to my words of hopelessness, of how he felt familiar feelings in 2006. He spoke of how he was so thankful he got the help he did because his life was full of joy. That life ended one year after my breakdown, in December, 2010. Galen committed suicide.

Like I said, Galen was a friend of many years. We met in Colorado in 1986 when Mark and I moved there as a young married couple. We went to church with Galen and his wife and just did life together. But Galen was more like a brother to me than a friend. We were very much alike. We both seemed to love and invest in others more than most. We hungered for more in our relationships, especially with that of our Lord. But, unfortunately, we also hurt more deeply than most. When we feel, it's to the core of our being, whether it is joy, pain, discouragement, compassion, or even shame. As Mark and I went through years of infertility, Galen walked that road with us, feeling our pain and loving us through it. During a healing service at church, Galen anointed me with oil and prayed that I would conceive a child. Tears rolled down his face as he prayed words with such compassion. A few weeks later, I found out that I was pregnant. Her name was Molly. He also would feel our indescribable pain when Molly was stillborn on the day she was due to bless us with her presence. I have a sweet suspicion that a precious little girl met Galen as he entered his haven of rest. And I know that he knew exactly who she was the moment he laid eyes upon her. What a blessing for this mother to envision that reunion.

I guess I'm not completely surprised that Galen and I shared this tragic path of life called depression. Although our situations bringing us to a point of desperation were obviously very different, our sense of hope at that crucial time was not. My heart breaks that he carried out his plan. I hurt to know that his pain reached a point that his broken mind couldn't see any other option.

I pray that Galen's family can forgive Galen for the pain he left them with and that they would realize that from the moment he made up his mind, it wasn't about them....it wasn't about his new grandbaby.....it wasn't even about His Lord. His mind shut down. No different than if his heart had given out, right? Then why does it feel so different to those left behind? Because it feels like a choice, a choice to leave them with the pain. It feels nothing short of selfish. But the truth is, there is nothing of 'self' left in the decision. To be honest, the mind is quite blank. It is void of emotion, it is void of any sense of judgment. I don't know exactly what took place in my friend's mind in the last hours of his life, but I do know his heart. He had the heart of Christ.

I will miss you, Galen. You have touched my life in so many ways. I will see you again, my friend. That I know for certain. I pray that an unexplainable peace will find its way into the years ahead for his family and that they will remember him for his life and not his death, for his joy and not his pain. He was a tender, gentle man of God that adored his family and his friends. I pray they never lose sight of that.

MY MAN...

I would love for my husband, Mark, to write a few words from his perspective. Fact is, he's never read my story. Not one word. He says that he can't relive those moments. He says he can't go back there in his mind, nor in his heart. It's just too fragile. It's too painful. So, I will write a few words about this man and what I watched him endure. I will write what it felt like to be loved unconditionally before, during, and after my breakdown. And if you are a spouse of one that is experiencing emotional and/or mental issues, I pray these words give you strength and hope.

Mark is not a real tender around the edges kind-of-guy. To tell you the truth, he's a little gruff. But there's also a side of him that I just can't get enough of. It's the side of him that doesn't give up on me; that believes in me when I struggle to believe in myself.

As I began to deal with hormone issues early on, Mark became my encourager to a degree I had never known him to be. He watched as my inner strength began to disappear and even though it was a trait that was unfamiliar, he became very good at holding me up, never allowing one ounce of dignity to slip from my grasp. When insecurities began to creep into my world, it was foreign to both of us. He knew me as confident and independent. It must have been horrifying to see the weakness prevail, wondering if this was his *new* wife, a woman he barely recognized at times. But he never clued me in on this inevitable fear. He simply held me more often, he frequently cried with me, and he interceded before our God for me. Simply put, he just loved me for who

I was at that moment and for who he knew me to be. I couldn't ask for more than that.

He would be the first to say that as my illness became worse and particularly during those last few weeks, as my hormones were spiraling out of control, he didn't know how to help me. He knew I needed more than he could give, but he didn't know whom to turn to. So, he did all he could and prayed that it would be enough. Because I was the one with the medical knowledge, he was waiting for cues from me. He got none.

If you are close to someone that is suffering, don't wait for them to *ask* for help. The fact is, they may need more help than they are aware of or are willing to admit. This realization hit Mark like a brick wall on the night of October 31st, finding empty pill bottles, certain of my intent to end my life. The intense fear that must have sucked the very breath from him at that moment! I heard that fear in his voice when he called me that night. Unfortunately, I did not have the mental capacity to respond in love to his pleas. That fear turned to anger as he realized he had been lied to and deceived by the very woman that he had poured himself into. He would tell me later that the days that followed were the hardest he would ever come to know. He struggled to make any sense of the fact that his wife would *choose* to end a life with him and with his children, that this one that he loved more than anything on this earth would orchestrate a plan that would have destroyed who he was as a man, a husband, and a father. He told me of gut-wrenching grief and endless tears that he cried during the hours that followed his arrival back home after leaving me that night. He watched his wife, with a look of terror that he's never seen on her, be placed into a security vehicle and transported to a lock-down psych facility. He shared of the pain he felt as he opened the satchel containing over 150 pills and the decision he'd made during those hours to flush several pills a day, the last one being flushed down the toilet the day I returned home from the psych facility. He explained to me that he did it in that way to remind him every day of my absence, what *might* have happened, but *didn't* happen. He made sure each and every one of the pills were gone by the time I got home, never again to revisit it, never to *throw it in my face*. And, he hasn't. He's never talked of the pain I caused him; of the devastation I would have created for him and our kids had my plan succeeded. He freed me of that guilt and shame. I carried enough guilt and shame on my own. I'm ever grateful that he didn't add to it.

To say that he has been and continues to be my rock is an understatement. He has prevailed when I didn't deserve his commitment. He has loved me unconditionally through seasons of life that most couples will never experience. I am humbled. I am grateful. And I am increasingly in love. Thank you, Mark, for loving me.....hormones and all!

HAPPY ANNIVERSARY!

October 31st comes around every year, ready or not. Some anniversaries are tougher than others. Most are days spent thanking the Lord for life, thanking Him for redemption, restoration, and healing. But on occasion, I have a tough one, remembering and struggling the events of that day and those that followed. A recent one brought about the following thoughts....

Why must I revisit the worst experience of my life? My Lord raised me, He transformed me, and He changed me. Is there more? *There's always more.* Did Lazarus have to go back to the tomb.....ever? Maybe not physically, but most likely he went back there mentally and emotionally many times. There were probably times when he thought, *I'm so grateful You raised me, You brought me back to life, but couldn't You have just healed me? Spared me from the tomb? When I was unwrapped 'in all my glory', there I stood; naked and uncertain as to what happened. I had a stench that I smelled for days and weeks. And what about the people that saw me like that? Will that vision of me truly ever go away? Will they be able to get that scene out of their head? Or will that always be a part of 'who I am'? When I look in the mirror, I still see the crease lines where the cloth was wrapped so tightly around my face and I'm reminded of the transformation that took place in that tomb; I'm reminded of the moment I heard the voice of my Lord speak life into my dead body; I'm reminded of the moment I heard the cries for joy when those that loved me knew I was alive. But, I'm also reminded of the sheer terror I felt the moment I breathed my first unexpected breath and I was in total darkness. I could hear His voice, but I couldn't see His face. It was cold and I couldn't move. Uncertain where I was, I was so scared. Then I heard His voice again. I recognized it. It was Jesus. He was telling me that it was going to be ok. I was alive. I would not die...not today. As He spoke, my fear and uncertainties left me. He began to remove the cloth from my face. It was dark, but I knew those eyes. They were His. I wasn't sure what got me in this dark, stench-filled placed, but at that very moment, it didn't matter. He was with me. As He sat me up and continued to unwrap my body, I realized that the second I step out of that tomb, things will never be the same. I would be changed.*

The memories are still so vivid. As Jesus and I approach the opening, I hesitate. I'm so nervous. I feel really exposed. I'm completely naked, I have pieces of cloth hanging off of me and I smell like death. The embarrassment is overwhelming. I wish I could've cleaned up before everyone saw me. I guess I can't help but wonder if the image they see today will ever completely leave them. Maybe it's not supposed to. Maybe it's ok for others to see me at my absolute worst; to view my imperfections, not one unexposed. What if they turn away in disgust? What if they can't see me at my worst, my weakest? What if they leave me standing there, naked, exposed, and stinking?
Fact is, I have no choice. There's only one way out. But I won't be walking out there alone. He's with me. I hear the Lord's voice in my ear, whispering so close that it causes

me to gasp. "It's ok, Lazarus, you will always remember this day, but you won't always feel the shame that you feel at this moment. I will heal you. And I will use this day for My glory. Trust Me, Lazarus."

So, I'm guessing you see the analogy. The memories will come. It's part of it. But, my God will use even the most painful memories for my good and for His glory. That makes for an anniversary worth celebrating!

Section Three:

Hope found through His Word

There are many scriptures and readings that I have clung to during my times of darkness and also times of healing. I hope they speak to you like they have me. There were many times that they literally breathed life into me.

Psalm 25:16
"Turn Yourself to me and have mercy on me, for I am desolate and afflicted. The troubles of my heart have enlarged. Bring me out of my distresses!"

Isaiah 60:1,2
"Arise, shine; for your light has come! And the glory of the Lord is risen upon you. For behold, darkness shall cover the earth, and deep darkness the people; but the Lord will arise over you and His glory will be seen upon you."

Isaiah 60: 19,20
"The sun shall no longer be your light by day, nor for brightness shall the moon give light to you, but the Lord will be to you an everlasting light, and your God your glory. Your sun shall no longer go down, nor shall your moon withdraw itself; for the Lord will be your everlasting light, and the days of your mourning shall be ended."

Isaiah 66:12
"Behold, I will extend peace to her like a river."

Malachi 3:10,11
"And try Me now in this, says the Lord, if I will not open for you the windows of heaven and pour out for you such blessing that there will not be room enough to receive it."
vs. 11 "And I will rebuke the devourer for your sakes, so that he will not destroy the fruit of your ground, nor shall the vine fail to bear fruit for you in the field."

Philippians 4:5
"Let your gentleness be known to all men. The Lord is at hand."

Job 22: 21,22
"Now acquaint yourself with Him and be at peace; thereby good will come to you. Receive instruction from His mouth, and lay up His words in your heart."

Psalm 27:13,14
"I would have lost heart, unless I had believed that I would see the goodness of the Lord in the land of the living. Wait on the Lord, be of good courage and He shall strengthen your heart; Wait, I say, on the Lord."

Psalm 31:9,10
"Have mercy on me, O Lord, for I am in trouble; my eye wastes away with grief, Yes, my soul and my body. My strength fails because of my iniquity, and my bones waste away." vs.14 "But as for me, I trust in You, O Lord; I say 'You are my God! My times are in your hand'".

Psalm 119:133
"Direct my steps by Your word, and let no iniquity have dominion over me."

Psalm 138:8
"The Lord will perfect that which concerns me, Your mercy, O Lord, endures forever; Do not forsake the works of Your hands."

Psalm 145:17-19
"The Lord is righteous in all His ways, gracious in all His works. The Lord is near to all who call upon Him, to all who call upon Him in truth, He will fulfill the desire of those who fear Him, He will also hear their cry and save them."

2 Samuel 22:2-7
"The Lord is my rock and my fortress and my deliverer; the God of my strength, in whom I will trust; my shield and the horn of my salvation, my stronghold and my refuge; my Savior, You save me from violence, I will call upon the Lord, who is worthy to be praised; so shall I be saved from my enemies; when the waves of death surround me, the snares of death confronted me, in my distress I called upon the Lord, and cried out to my God; He heard my voice from His temple, and my cry entered His ears."

Joshua 3:5
"Sanctify yourselves, for tomorrow the Lord will do wonders among you."

Romans 9:17
"For this very purpose I have raised you up, that I may show My power in you, and that My name may be declared in all the earth."

Jeremiah 29:11,12
"For I know the thoughts that I think toward you, says the Lord, thoughts of peace and not of evil, to give you a future and a hope. Then you will call upon Me and go and pray to Me, and I will listen to you. You will seek me and find me."

Habakkuk 1:5
"Be utterly astounded! For I will work a work in your days which you would not believe, though it were told to you."

Isaiah 32:16-19
"Then justice will dwell in the wilderness and righteousness remain in the fruitful field. The work of righteousness will be peace, the effect of righteousness, quietness and assurance forever. My people will dwell in a peaceful habitation, in secure dwellings, and in quiet resting places, though hail comes down on the forest, and the city is brought low in humiliation."

Isaiah 41:9,10
"You are my servant, I have chosen you and have not cast you away. Fear not, for I am with you. Be not dismayed, for I am your God, I will strengthen you. Yes, I will help you. I will uphold you with my righteous right hand."

Isaiah 40:28-31
"Have you not known? Have you not heard? The everlasting God, the Lord, the Creator of the ends of the earth, neither faints nor is weary, His understanding is unsearchable. He gives power to the weak, and to those who have no might He

increases strength. Even the youths shall faint and be weary, and the young men shall utterly fall, but those who wait on the Lord shall renew their strength; they shall mount up with wings like eagles, they shall run and not be weary, they shall walk and not faint."

Isaiah 43:2,3
"Fear not, for I have redeemed you; I have called you by your name; You are mine. When you pass through the waters, I will be with you, and through the rivers, they shall not overflow you. When you walk through the fire, you shall not be burned. Nor shall the flame scorch you. For I am the Lord your God, the Holy One of Israel, your Savior."

Isaiah 43:18,19
"Do not remember the former things, nor consider the things of old. Behold I will do a new thing, now it shall spring forth; shall you not know it? I will even make a road in the wilderness and rivers in the desert."

Psalm 25:20,21
"Keep my soul and deliver me; Let me not be ashamed, for I put my trust in You. Let integrity and uprightness preserve me, for I wait for You."

Psalm 27:7-10
"Hear, O Lord, when I cry with my voice! Have mercy upon me, and answer me. When you said, seek my face, my heart said to You, 'Your face, Lord, will I seek'. Do not turn Your servant away in anger, You have been my help; do not leave me nor forsake me, O God of my salvation. When my father and my mother forsake me, then the Lord will take care of me."

From My Utmost for His Highest[1]:
"Has God trusted you with His silence...a silence that has great meaning? Can God trust you with it or are you still asking Him for a visible answer? God will give you the very blessing you ask if you refuse to go any further without the,

but His silence is the sign that He is bringing you into an even more wonderful understanding of Himself. Allow Him to give you the first sign of His intimacy....silence." (10/11)

"Are you alone at your 'Jordan River'? The Jordan River represents the type of separation where you have no fellowship with anyone else. You have been to the Jordan over and over with your Elijah, but now you are facing it alone. There is no use in saying that you cannot go, the experience is here, and you must go. If you truly want to know whether or not God is the God your faith believes Him to be, then go through your 'Jordan' alone."

"At your 'Bethel', you will find yourself at your wits' end but at the beginning of God's wisdom. When you come to your wits' end and you feel inclined to panic-don't! Stand true to God and He will bring out His truth in a way that will make your life an expression of worship." (8/11)

"Are you prepared to let God take you into total oneness with Himself, paying no more attention to what you call the great things of life? Once you totally surrender, you will no longer think about what God is going to do. Abandonment to Him means to refuse yourself the luxury of asking questions. If you totally surrender yourself to God, He says, 'I will give your life to you as a prize.'" (4/28)

From "Finding Favor with the King$_2$"

"Will you dangle your toes over the edge of God's promises and leap out into the unknown, casting your fate upon the faithfulness of God?"

"Just remember that the more important your future, the greater your opponent! Do you suddenly feel as if you are facing giant enemies? Hold on! Your destiny is about to be revealed. If it had not been for an enemy called 'Goliath', David would always have been just a shepherd."

"When destiny pushes you to the edge of desperation and the limits of your abilities, cast your future into the hands of God and take a big leap of faith!"

References

1. *My Utmost for His Highest: An Updated Edition in Today's Language.* Chicago: Moody, 1997. Print.

2. *Finding Favor with the King: Preparing for Your Moment in His Presence.* Minneapolis, MN: Bethany House, 2003. Print.

Made in the USA
Charleston, SC
04 December 2015